SONATAS AND SUITES, OPUS 8

Part I

RECENT RESEARCHES IN THE MUSIC OF THE BAROQUE ERA

Robert L. Marshall, general editor

A-R Editions, Inc., publishes six quarterly series—

Recent Researches in the Music of the Middle Ages and Early Renaissance
Margaret Bent, general editor

Recent Researches in the Music of the Renaissance
James Haar, general editor

Recent Researches in the Music of the Baroque Era
Robert L. Marshall, general editor

Recent Researches in the Music of the Classical Era
Eugene K. Wolf, general editor

Recent Researches in the Music of the Nineteenth and Early Twentieth Centuries
Rufus Hallmark, general editor

Recent Researches in American Music
H. Wiley Hitchcock, general editor—

which make public music that is being brought to light
in the course of current musicological research.

Each volume in the *Recent Researches* is devoted
to works by a single composer or to a single genre of composition,
chosen because of its potential interest to scholars and performers,
and prepared for publication according to the standards that govern
the making of all reliable historical editions.

Subscribers to this series, as well as patrons of subscribing institutions,
are invited to apply for information about the "Copyright-Sharing Policy"
of A-R Editions, Inc., under which the contents of this volume
may be reproduced free of charge for study or performance.

Correspondence should be addressed:

A-R EDITIONS, INC.
315 West Gorham Street
Madison, Wisconsin 53703

RECENT RESEARCHES IN THE MUSIC OF THE BAROQUE ERA • VOLUME LI

Tomaso Albinoni

SONATAS AND SUITES, OPUS 8

For Two Violins, Violoncello, and Basso Continuo

Part I

Edited by C. David Harris

A-R EDITIONS, INC. • MADISON

All inquiries regarding performance and recording rights should be addressed to the publisher.

Performance parts are available from the publisher.

© 1986 by A-R Editions, Inc.
All rights reserved
Printed in the United States of America

Library of Congress Cataloging-in-Publication Data

Albinoni, Tomaso, 1671–1750.
 [Baletti e sonate, violins (2), continuo, op. 8]
 Sonatas and suites, opus 8, for two violins,
violoncello, and basso continuo.

 (Recent researches in the music of the Baroque era,
ISSN 0484-0828 ; v. 51–52)
 Figured bass realized for keyboard instrument.
 Includes bibliographical references.
 1. Trio-sonatas (Violins (2), continuo)—Scores.
2. Suites (Violins (2), continuo)—Scores. I. Harris,
C. David. II. Series.
M2.R238   vol. 51–52   [M312.4]   86-750000
ISBN 0-89579-207-9 (pbk. : v. 1)
ISBN 0-89579-208-7 (pbk. : v. 2)

Contents

Part I

Preface
   The Composer   vii
   The Music   vii
   The Edition   viii
   Notes on Performance   ix
   Critical Notes   ix
   Acknowledgments   x
   Notes   xi
Plate I   xii
Plate II   xiii

Sonata I   1

Suite I   19

Sonata II   29

Suite II   56

Sonata III   66

Suite III   92

Preface

The sonatas and suites of Tomaso Albinoni's Opus 8 are published here for the first time complete in a modern edition.[1] Because of the canonic content of the sonatas, the opus represents the most ambitious collection of chamber music composed by Albinoni. Albinoni took particular pride in the compositional achievement of Opus 8: a fusion of the lyricism inspired both by Corelli's sonatas and the *bel canto* style with the contrapuntal rigor exemplified by Giovanni Battista Vitali's canonic works.

Albinoni's Opus 8 was published as a set of four parts by Jeanne Roger, Amsterdam, ca. 1722 (RISM A 737). It was dedicated to Count Christian Heinrich von Watzdorf, Polish court counselor, who, at the time, was living in Rome.[2] Sometime after 1722 the edition was reissued (RISM A 736), with no alterations except for the substitution of "Estienne Roger & Le Cene" for "Jeanne Roger" on the title page (see Plate I).[3] The Jeanne Roger print apparently survives complete only in the Sächsische Landesbibliothek, Dresden (Mus. 2199-Q-6). A complete exemplar of the reissue by Estienne Roger & Le Cène survives in the Library of Congress (M402.A2A35). The present editor has compared this exemplar with a microfilm copy of the Dresden exemplar; because of the accessibility of the Washington exemplar, it has served as the source for the present edition.

The Composer

Tomaso Albinoni was born in Venice in 1671 and died there in 1751 (1750, Venetian calendar). Little is known about his early years. Although it is thought that he may have studied with Giovanni Legrenzi, the leading Venetian composer of instrumental music in the late seventeenth century, there is no proof of this. His family's comfortable circumstances allowed Albinoni to devote himself to music during his youth; he described himself as *dilettante veneto* in early publications. Although Tomaso, as eldest son, would have inherited the family business upon the death of his father in 1709, he chose instead to pursue an independent career in music. After 1710 he referred to himself as *musico di violino*.

It was principally his instrumental music that spread Albinoni's fame over much of Europe; more than 140 instrumental works, most of them published during his lifetime, survive. Albinoni's activities in Venice, however, centered on opera: he may have written eighty-one operas, of which "something over 50 'public' operas are known from librettos or the few scores that have survived."[4] Among these was the first Venetian opera on a libretto by Metastasio: *La Didone abbandonata*, given its premiere at San Cassiano in 1725.[5] Although Albinoni composed most of his operas for Venice, some were written for other Italian cities, including Florence, Rome, Genoa, Milan, Bologna, and Ferrara. One of the operas for Florence, *La Griselda*, is the first of Albinoni's settings of librettos by Zeno. For this production, in 1703, Albinoni left his native city, as he did also in 1722 for the premieres of *I veri amici* and *Il trionfo d'Amore*, presented in Munich during the wedding festivities for Karl Albert, prince-elector. Albinoni continued to compose until about 1741, when his last opera, *Artamene*, was produced in Venice.

Ten numbered sets of instrumental works by Albinoni first appeared in print between 1694 and about 1735. Two unnumbered sets and single works in collections also were published; various other collections and individual works remain in manuscript. The published sets include solo sonatas and trio sonatas in the church sonata tradition, chamber sonatas or suites (called *balletti*), and sinfonias and concertos.[6] Among the transalpine musicians who knew certain of these works was J. S. Bach, who composed fugues (BWV 946, 950, 951, 951a)[7] on subjects from Albinoni's Opus 1 and corrected the bass realization for Opus 6, no. 6, made by Heinrich Nikolaus Gerber, his pupil.

The Music

As indicated above, the style of Albinoni's sonatas demonstrates two primary traits of Italian chamber music from the decades around 1700: the expansive lyricism first brought to a peak by Corelli and the contrapuntal textures that occasionally crystallized in canonic writing, as in the music of Vitali. The style of Corelli remained the standard and reference point for many composers of Albinoni's generation. Albinoni himself imitated various of Corelli's stylistic procedures and adopted the slow-fast-slow-fast order of movements in Corelli's Opp. 1 and 3.[8] Soon after they first were issued, Corelli's works were republished in Venice, as well as in other Italian cities, and thus they would have been accessible to the young Albinoni. In addition, Albinoni may have known certain of the collections containing canons that had appeared in northern Italy during the seventeenth century. These include G. B. Buonamente's *Settimo libro di sonate, sinfonie, gagliarde, corrente, et brandi* (1637); Marco Uccellini's *Sonate, arie et corrente*, [*libro III*] (1642) and *Sonate, over canzoni*, Opus 5 (1649); G. M. Bononcini's Opus 3 (1669); and, above all, Vitali's *Artificii musicali* (1689), the most ambitious and most famous of all of these collections. Vitali's preface to this set must have posed the ultimate challenge to an aspiring young composer of that time.

> He who does not know how to manage the most profound secrets of the Art does not deserve the title of musician. . . . I have observed [that]—scattered in various compositions by the most virtuoso of men who ever com-

bined Notes, who, longing to make their names immortal, dedicated themselves to these laborious tasks, deeming that, without these one cannot attain the title of perfect composer—canons effectively are the true test of counterpoint.[9]

Albinoni rose to this challenge in the fast movements of his sonatas in Opus 8, where the violins play in canon at the unison, accompanied by a bass that is, for the most part, free. At times, however, the bass imitates the violins, a procedure that Albinoni claimed to have invented. In his own preface to Opus 8 he also stressed the considerable effort that composition of the canons required.

> Well you know, gracious and indulgent reader, that in the many Works that I held up to the public eye so as to amuse you, if ever I became tiresome with my remonstrances, your ingrained Approval gave me Impetus and Courage therein. But in this Work, which, more than any other, cost me both Study and Toil, I cannot help but implore you for a special and persistent Indulgence. If at other times I obtained it from your kind nature, this time your generous Justice owes it to me; for who does not understand the great Diligence that Canons require—moreover, Canons with some gracious singing style, and even more the introduction of subjects proposed by the Violins into the Bass—adapted to the Method and to the length of sonatas. I would like to believe (inasmuch as I have not seen such by anyone) that I am the first Inventor of this style, and, if that be so, I should like also to hope that such a toil, once undertaken, might bring me some small measure of honor, at least with the most knowledgeable. And because I am aware that going from one Canon to another could, perhaps, cause you a little weariness with regard to the same Method, I took the expedient of inserting after each one of these Canons some other Composition of a different taste and style, just as Intermezzi are mingled between the acts of Tragedies. Which might succeed with regard to your delight, I would not be able to say. I hope, however, for no less Enjoyment in you for this work, over which I toiled more than for any other Works of mine which you received with such great and generous goodness. Read, play, consider at length, and live happily.[10]

Since Albinoni's sonatas generally correspond to the slow-fast-slow-fast order of movements of the church sonata, the canons appear in the second and fourth movements, except for the first sonata, which has three movements in the order fast-slow-fast. It has been suggested that Albinoni may have wanted to present at the very outset of the collection a movement that would demonstrate the essential stylistic feature of the opus, and thus he dispensed with the customary slow first movement.[11] In this opening movement, *comes* follows *dux* at a distance of two measures, and Albinoni articulated the flow of the music with frequent cadences. Subsequent canonic movements show Albinoni's increasing mastery of the technique: the space between the canonic voices is larger, and cadencing is less frequent.

When the bass remains independent of the canons, Albinoni's procedure corresponds to the method that J. S. Bach would use in most of the canons in the *Goldberg Variations*. When, however, the bass imitates the violins and renders the texture momentarily fugal, the compositional technique corresponds to that which Bach would employ in the *"Fuga canonica"* of the *Musical Offering*.

While Albinoni aimed expressly for a "gracious singing style" in the canons, he achieved this more readily in the slow movements of the sonatas. These attain, at times, a heightened expressiveness, with more chromaticism and with modulation more fluent than in the canonic fast movements.

Albinoni used the title "sonata" for his works of the type that, before 1700, had been called *sonata da chiesa*. For works corresponding to the *sonata da camera*, or suite, he used the term *balletto*, as had other composers, for example, Maurizio Cazzati (Op. 15, 1654). Although Albinoni, or his publisher, introduced conspicuous titles for the sonatas, the *balletti* (spelled *"baletti"* on the title page of the source and labeled "suites" in this edition) follow the individual sonatas in the Jeanne Roger and Roger and Le Cène prints with no special designation other than an Arabic numeral after the word Allemanda. To include sonatas and suites of dances within the same opus was hardly new. Various composers previously had grouped these by genre, if not in alternation, for example, Cazzati (Op. 15), Legrenzi (Op. 4, 1656), Bononcini (Op. 3, 1669), Agostino Guerrieri (Op. 1, 1673), Giovanni Battista Gigli (Op. 1, 1690), T. A. Vitali (Op. 4, 1701), and F. M. Veracini (Op. 1, ca. 1720).[12] Each of the *balletti* in Albinoni's Opus 8 comprises three dances beginning with an *allemanda* and continuing with various others: *corrente* and *gavotta* or *giga* and *sarabanda*. Similar groupings of dances had appeared in Albinoni's Opus 3 (1701).

The lyricism cited by Albinoni in his discussion of the sonatas appears also in the suites. In these, the first violin typically predominates, while the second violin, cello, and basso continuo convey either simple harmonic support or counterpoint that also defines the harmony. Imitation often appears at the outset of sections, but it soon dissolves into a less specific texture. The dances, all in binary form except for the three-section Gavotta in Suite VI, observe the harmonic plan characteristic of baroque dances: movement toward the dominant within the first section and a return to the tonic, often with a subsidiary cadence on the mediant or submediant, during the second section. The first two sections of the Gavotta in Suite VI modulate to the dominant and the mediant, respectively, and the return to the tonic appears in the third section.

The Edition

This edition of Albinoni's Opus 8 is based on the print published, in partbook format, in Amsterdam by Roger and Le Cène and preserved in the Library of Congress. As stated above, the *balletti* bear minimal identification in this print. However, in view of their musical independence from the sonatas, these pieces are treated here as separate works and entitled "suites," which identifies them at once for the modern musician as collections of dances. Their placement in relation to the individual sonatas has been retained.

Although the cello and the continuo have separate partbooks in the source, these parts are largely the same. They have been combined in the present edition, and where the cello part deviates from the bass part, the cello notes are stemmed up.

Albinoni's practice concerning accidentals involves several basic factors. (1) In the figured bass, often there is no accidental affecting the third above the bass; instead, the local context and the contour of the bass indicate whether a major or a minor third is required. (2) In dominant chords, either of the prevailing tonality or within a departure from it, thirds are necessarily major and are not always indicated by figures. (3) When, in the minor mode, a figure calls for a major third, it follows that the fifth above the bass will be perfect, even though this is not indicated by a figure. (4) In the minor mode, a raised seventh degree implies that the sixth degree adjacent to it will be raised to avoid a melodic augmented second. In the edition, accidentals have been supplied tacitly in all of these situations. Leading-tones without figures in the bass part have been realized as first-inversion dominant chords. No figures have been added to the figured bass part in the situations discussed above, although there are a few instances of editorially added or altered figures in other situations. Added figures are enclosed in square brackets; altered figures are enclosed in square brackets and/or cited in the Critical Notes.

Editorial accidentals, rests, dynamic markings, and trill symbols are enclosed within square brackets; editorial cautionary accidentals are enclosed within parentheses. Editorial trills have been suggested for cadential situations where the third and fifth appear over a dominant tone in the bass. While Albinoni often specified trills, they sometimes are lacking at cadences. Editorial trill signs thus are supplied in order to compensate for what may have been a casual attitude toward their indication or, perhaps, for the tacit expectation that performers would know to add trills in these situations.

Piano and *forte*, always written out in full in the source, have been abbreviated to *p* and *f*. In general, the beaming of notes has been modernized where the archaic beaming in the source appears to have no significance for performance. When a tied note in the bass bearing a change of figure appears in situations where a dot or a larger single note could have achieved the same value, the notation of the source has been preserved.

Editorial slurs are represented by broken curves; these have been supplied to facilitate agreement of bowings in canonic passages, in parallel passages, and in passages where the violins play comparable motives simultaneously. These slurs have been supplied sparingly, with the rationale of aiding performers who may be playing from partbooks. In the present edition, several slurs, such as those for the second violin in measure 13 of the Allemanda in Suite IV, suggest possible emendation to patterns comprising three slurred sixteenth-notes, but because these same patterns of pitches are slurred in contrasting ways elsewhere in the movement, the slurs in measure 13 have been left as they appear in the source. In the Giga of Suite I, however, it seemed advisable to emend the slurring of the sixteenth-note patterns in measures 2–7 to conform to the pattern announced by the first violin in measure 1: ♫. In measure 2, the source gives the second violin, playing for the moment in canon with the first violin, the pattern ♫ ; this slurring seems unlikely, not only because of the canonic imitation but also because of the tempo of the movement. Further justification for emendation can be found in the Giga of Suite III, where groups of four sixteenth-notes in a similar rhythmic context always are slurred together.

The realization of the figured bass, given here in cue-size notation, has been kept simple, experience showing that it is much easier for the performer to amplify and embellish a spare accompaniment than to prune one that is excessively florid. Moreover, a simple accompaniment would be suitable for organ, the instrument actually specified in the bass part of the source, although the source's title page calls for harpsichord.

Notes on Performance

Although they are not indicated in the present edition, there are various instances where notated rhythms might be adjusted to conform to those of another part that has smaller note values. In the Corrente of Suite II, for example, the first violinist might delay and shorten the eighth-notes of measures 4 and 13 so that they will coincide with the sixteenth-notes in the second violin part. In this same movement, the pattern dotted eighth-note, sixteenth-note might at times be softened to form a long-short triplet that would concur with triplet rhythms in another part.[13]

Most trills will sound better with an upper-note beginning, emphasizing the initial dissonance thus created with the lower part or parts, and many trills can be connected to the following note with a suffix using the lower neighbor and main note or with an anticipation of the following note after a stop on the main note. Because Albinoni's dynamic markings sometimes appear within phrases rather than at breaks in the music, some of them may have been intended to represent goals of *crescendo* and *decrescendo* rather than terraced effects.[14]

Critical Notes

The critical notes document discrepancies between the source (the Roger and Le Cène print) and the present edition. Pitches are given according to the familiar system, wherein c′ = middle C, c″ = the C above middle C, and so forth. Abbreviations used below are as follows: vn. = violin; vc. = cello; b.c. = basso continuo; m. = measure.

In general, the canons in the sonatas are maintained strictly, but occasional deviations appear in Sonatas II–VI. A few of these deviations can be attributed to errors in engraving the source; they have been emended in the present edition and are accounted for in the individual entries below. Other deviations, however, serve a compositional purpose, as when the *comes* offers a brief variation on the *dux* (Sonata IV, Allegro [fourth movement], m. 24/33 and m. 57/66; Sonata V, Allegro [second movement], m. 35/42), or when an adjustment in the *comes* accommodates the harmonic context of the moment (Sonata IV, Allegro [fourth movement], m. 40/49; Sonata VI, Allegro [second movement], m. 32/41). In Sonata II, Allegro (second movement), m. 4/12 and m. 100/108, it seems unlikely that the deviation concerns an engraving error, since the G-sharp, which was not in the original key signature, had to be engraved in different places for *dux* and *comes*; therefore, this source reading has been allowed to stand.

Sonata I

Allegretto—M. 109, vn. II, note 1 is c″.

Suite I

Giga—M. 1, vn. II, anacrusis to this m. is eighth-rest. Mm. 2–7, vns. I and II, all sixteenth-notes have the slurring pattern ♪♬, emended by analogy with vn. parts in mm. 1, 9, and 14 and with the slurring of sixteenth-notes in the Giga of Suite III. M. 3, b.c., note 2, not note 3, has figure 6. M. 29, b.c., note 6 has figure ♮6.

Sarabanda—M. 18, vn. I, *p* begins with note 1. M. 32, vn. II, note 5 is d″ (emended by analogy with pattern in vn. II of m. 30).

Sonata II

Grave—M. 2, vn. II, last two notes are eighth-notes.

Allegro (fourth movement)—Mm. 39 and 169, vn. II, notes 2 and 3 are eighth-notes.

Suite II

Allemanda—M. 1, vn. II and b.c., anacrusis to this m. is eighth-rest.

Corrente—Mm. 21 and 42, vc. lacks slurs. M. 55, vn. I, note 2 is c″ (emended by analogy with m. 27).

Gavotta—M. 33, vn. II, *p* begins with note 1 of this m., not in m. 32. M. 35, vn. I, *f* begins with note 3 of this m., not in m. 34; vn. II, *f* begins with note 1 of this m., not in m. 34.

Sonata III

Larghetto—M. 31, vns. I and II, *p* begins with note 2.

Suite III

Allemanda—M. 1, b.c. and vc., anacrusis to this m. is eighth-rest.

Giga—M. 16, vn. II, *p* begins with note 1. M. 32, vn. I, *p* begins with note 1. M. 34, vns. I and II, superfluous quarter- and eighth-rests after note 3.

Sarabanda—M. 23, vn. II, note 4 is quarter-note and note 5 is eighth-note.

Sonata IV

Grave—M. 32, vn. II, notes 1 and 2 are quarter-notes.

Allegro (second movement)—M. 26, vc., note 3 is dotted quarter-note.

Allegro (fourth movement)—M. 5, b.c., note 2 has figures 7 6. M. 36, b.c., note 4 is eighth-note. M. 62, vn. II, note 1 is eighth-note and note 2 is lacking; emended by analogy with vn. I, m. 53. M. 68, b.c., note 2 has figures 7 6.

Suite IV

Sarabanda—M. 2, vc., note 1 is quarter-note and note 2 is eighth-note.

Sonata V

Allegro (fourth movement)—M. 64, vn. II, note 1 is eighth-note, notes 2 and 3 are sixteenth-notes. M. 66, vn. II, note 5 is a′.

Suite V

Allemanda—M. 11, vn. II, note 4 is not sharped. M. 25, vn. II, last note is d″-natural. M. 36, vn. II, note 1 is b′.

Corrente—Mm. 8, 10, and 11, vc. lacks slurs for the triplets.

Sonata VI

Grave—M. 3, b.c., note 1 has the figure ♮ and note 6 has the figure ♮7/5, and notes 8 and 9 are quarter-notes.

Allegro (second movement)—M. 75, vn. II, notes 7 and 8 are sixteenth-notes, note 9 is eighth-note. M. 119, b.c., note 1 has the figure ♮6/4.

Larghetto—M. 26, b.c., note 2, not note 3, has the figure 6.

Allegro (fourth movement)—M. 27, vn. II, note 1 is c″. M. 55, vn. I, note 4 is c″. M. 128, vn. II, note 5 is b′-flat. M. 139, vn. I, note 1 is eighth-note, notes 2 and 3 are sixteenth-notes. M. 149, vn. I, note 5 is b′-natural (emended by analogy with m. 164, vn. II). M. 174, b.c., note 2 is c. M. 196, vn. I and b.c. have whole-note, even though vn. II and vc. have half-note at this point.

Suite VI

Allemanda—M. 7, vn. I, the first double stop has e′-flat as quarter-note. M. 35, b.c., note 6 has the figure ♮4/2. M. 38, vn. I, the double stop has e′-flat as a quarter note.

Acknowledgments

The editor wishes to thank the Library of Congress for making available photocopies of the source and the plates used in the present edition; the Sächsische Landesbibliothek, Dresden, for providing a microfilm of the Jeanne Roger print of Albinoni's Opus 8; and Robert L. Marshall, general editor, for his assistance in various aspects of the edition. The editor also wishes to express appreciation to Drake University for a summer research grant and other support, and to Professor Joseph LaCava for assistance in the translation of Italian texts.

C. David Harris

Notes

1. Sonata I, Suite I, Sonata IV, and Suite IV have appeared in modern editions, however. See Tomaso Albinoni, *Balletto e sonata a tre*, ed. Frederick Polnauer (Bryn Mawr: Theodore Presser, 1977) for Sonata I and Suite I. See Tomaso Albinoni, *Sonata da chiesa a tre per due violini, violoncello e basso continuo, op. VIII/4a* and *Sonata da camera a tre per due violini, violoncello e basso continuo, op. VIII/4b*, ed. Erich Schenk (Vienna: Österreichische Bundesverlag, 1952; reprint, Vienna: Doblinger, 1969).

2. For a discussion of Watzdorf, see Michael Talbot, *Albinoni. Leben und Werk* (Adliswil: Edition Kunzelmann, 1980), p. 48.

3. Since only the Jeanne Roger print is cited as late as 1737 in the catalog of Roger & Le Cène, the reissue may have appeared after this date: see François Lesure, ed., *Bibliographie des éditions musicales publiées par Estienne Roger et Michel-Charles Le Cène (Amsterdam 1696–1743)*, Publications de la Société française de musicologie, 2d series, vol. 12 (Paris: Heugel, 1969).

4. *The New Grove Dictionary of Music and Musicians*, s.v. "Albinoni, Tomaso Giovanni," by Michael Talbot.

5. *Die Musik in Geschichte und Gegenwart*, s.v. "Albinoni," by Bernhard Paumgartner.

6. For a survey of Albinoni's instrumental works, see William S. Newman, "The Sonatas of Albinoni and Vivaldi," *Journal of the American Musicological Society* 5 (Summer 1952): 99–113, and, especially, Talbot, *Albinoni. Leben und Werk*.

7. Talbot, "Albinoni, Tomaso Giovanni."

8. William S. Newman, *The Sonata in the Baroque Era*, rev. ed. (Chapel Hill: The University of North Carolina Press, 1966), p. 166.

9. "Non merita il nome di musico chi non sa maneggiare in qualsivoglia modo gli arcani più profondi dell'Arte. . . . ho osservato sparsi in varie composizioni d'huomini i più virtuosi che mai intrecciassero Note che bramando rendere il nome immortale, si diedero a queste laboriose fatiche stimando senza queste non poter conseguire il nome di perfetto compositore per essere i Canoni realmente il vero esame del contrappunto." This quotation is taken from Remo Giazotto, *Tomaso Albinoni* (Milan: Fratelli Bocca, 1945), p. 190; translated here by Joseph LaCava.

10. "Tu ben sai benigno, e benevolo lettore in tante Opere, ch'esposi alla luce per riorcarli, se mai mi feci importuno con mie proteste, che già il tuo inveterato Aggradimento me ne dava Impulso, e Coraggio. Ma in questa Opera, che più d'ogn'altra mi costa e Studio, e Fatica, non posso a meno di non pregarti d'un particolare non tenue Compatimento. Se altre volte l'ottenni dalla tua ben' inclinata natura questa mel deve la tua generosa Giustizia; mentre chi non vede il grande Impegno, che sia campor Canoni: di più; canoni con qualche grazioso modo di cantare, e molto più per condure li soggetti proposti dalli Violini nel Basso e ridotti al Metado et alla lunghezza delle suonate: Vorrei credere (già che oio non vidi da alcuno) d'esser io il primo Inventore di questo modo, e se ciò fosse, vorrei anco sperare che una tale fatica intrapresa mi potesse recare qualche poco d'onore, almeno da i più intendenti. E perche conobbi che il passare da un Canone all'altro ti poteva forse dar un po di noia a riguardo dello stesso Metodo presi espediente d'intrecciare doppo di ciasch'uno d'essi Canoni qualche altro Componimento di gusto e stile diverso, come appunto trà gl'atti delle Tragedie si frameschiono gl'Intermezzi. Quali possono riuscire circa la tua dilettatione, saper non lo posso. Spero pero non minore in te il Gradimento per questa che più faticai, che nelle altre mie Opere che con si grande generosa bontà tu accogliesti. Leggi suona considera bene, e vivi felice." Translated here by Joseph LaCava.

11. Giazotto, *Tomaso Albinoni*, p. 189. To Talbot, however, the lack of an opening slow movement suggests the influence of the concerto; cf. *Albinoni. Leben und Werk*, p. 106.

12. Concerning the date of Veracini's Opus 1, see Newman, *The Sonata in the Baroque Era*, p. 184, n. 81.

13. For a discussion of the problems of dotted notes and triplets, see David D. Boyden, *The History of Violin Playing* (London: Oxford University Press, 1965), pp. 295–302 and 478–84.

14. David D. Boyden, "Dynamics in Seventeenth- and Eighteenth-Century Music," *Essays on Music in Honor of Archibald Thompson Davison* (Cambridge: Harvard University Press, 1957), pp. 186–93.

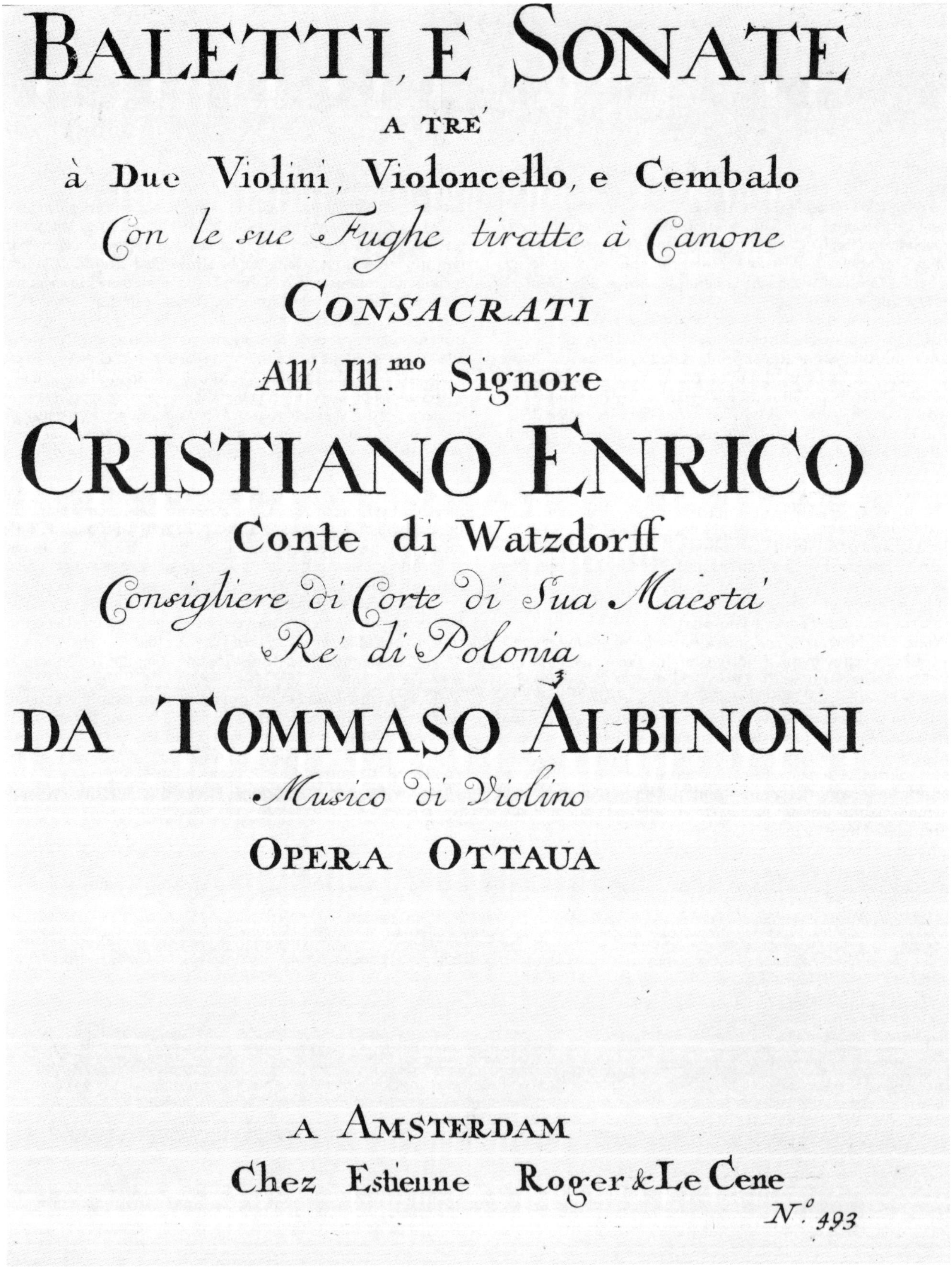

BALETTI, E SONATE

A TRE'

à Due Violini, Violoncello, e Cembalo

Con le sue Fughe tiratte à Canone

CONSACRATI

All' Ill.mo Signore

CRISTIANO ENRICO

Conte di Watzdorff

Consigliere di Corte di Sua Maestà
Re' di Polonia

DA TOMMASO ALBINONI

Musico di Violino

OPERA OTTAUA

A AMSTERDAM

Chez Estienne Roger & Le Cene

N.º 493

Plate I. Tomaso Albinoni, Opus 8, title page of violino primo part,
from the print issued by Roger and Le Cène, after 1722. Source size 23 × 29.5 cm.
(Courtesy Library of Congress, Washington, D.C.)

Plate II. Tomaso Albinoni, Opus 8, Sonata I, first page of violino primo part, from the print issued by Roger and Le Cène, after 1722. Source size 23 × 29.5 cm. (Courtesy Library of Congress, Washington, D.C.)

Sonata I

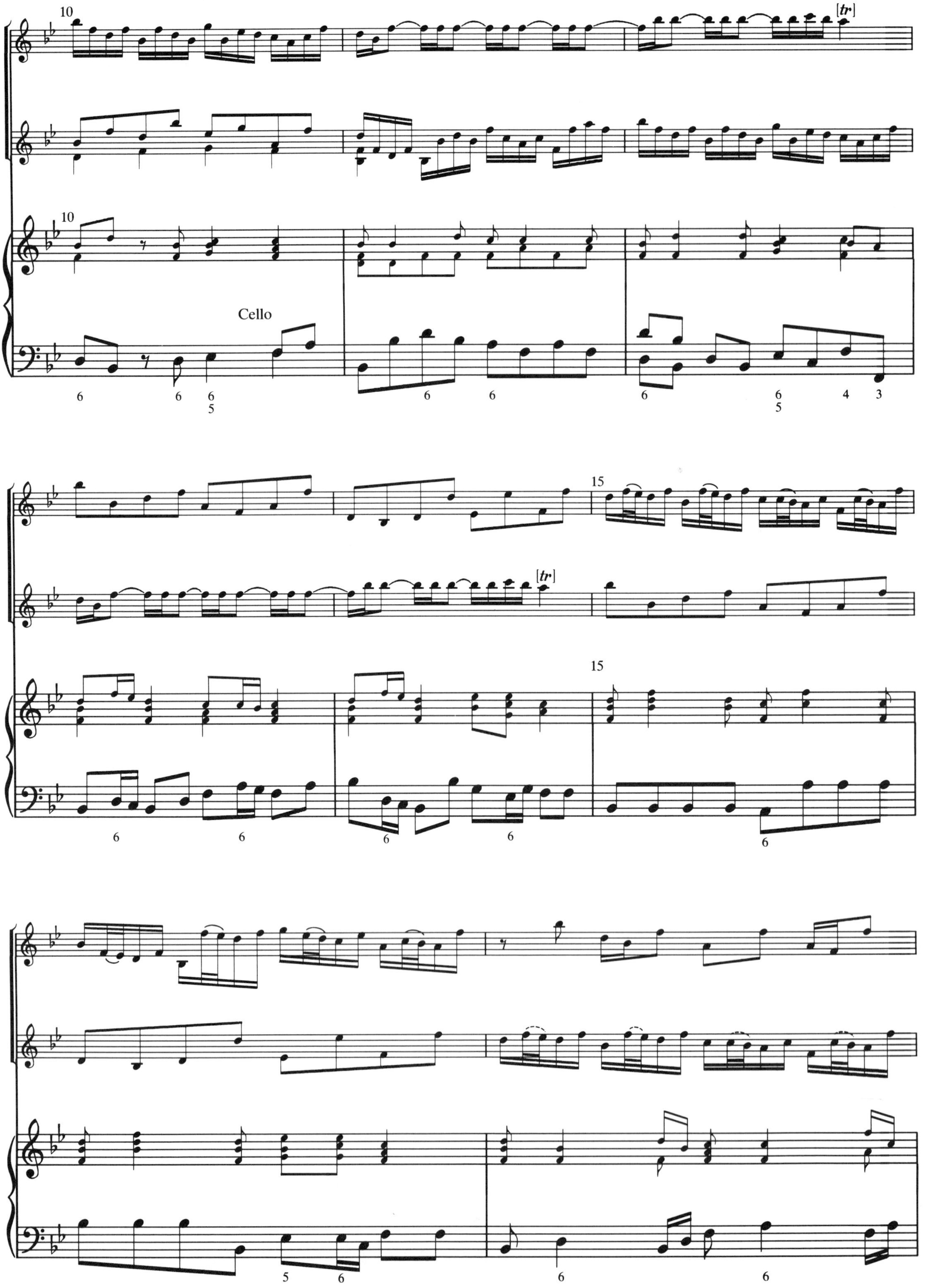

10
[tr]
Cello
15
[tr]

3

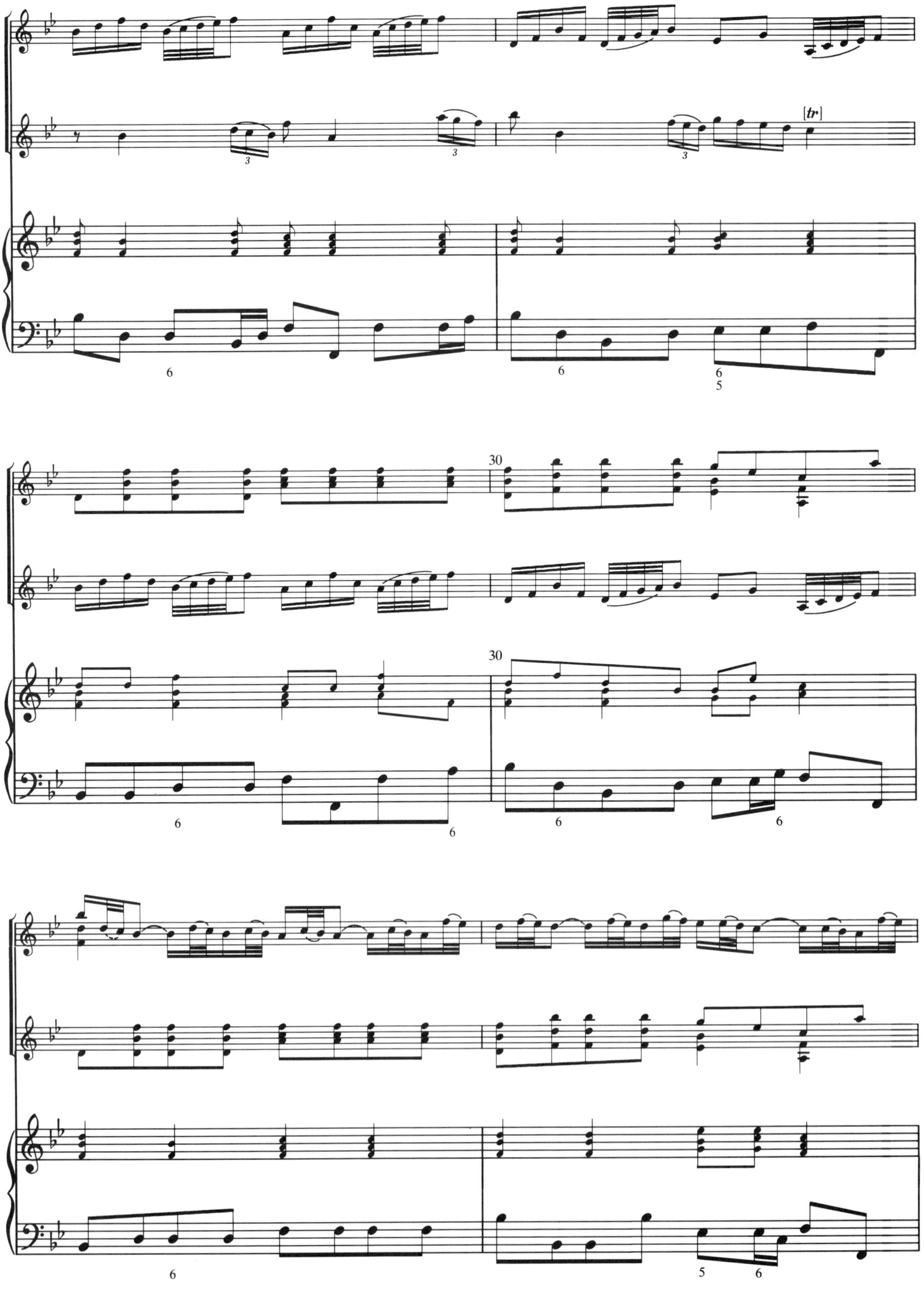
[tr]
30
30

5

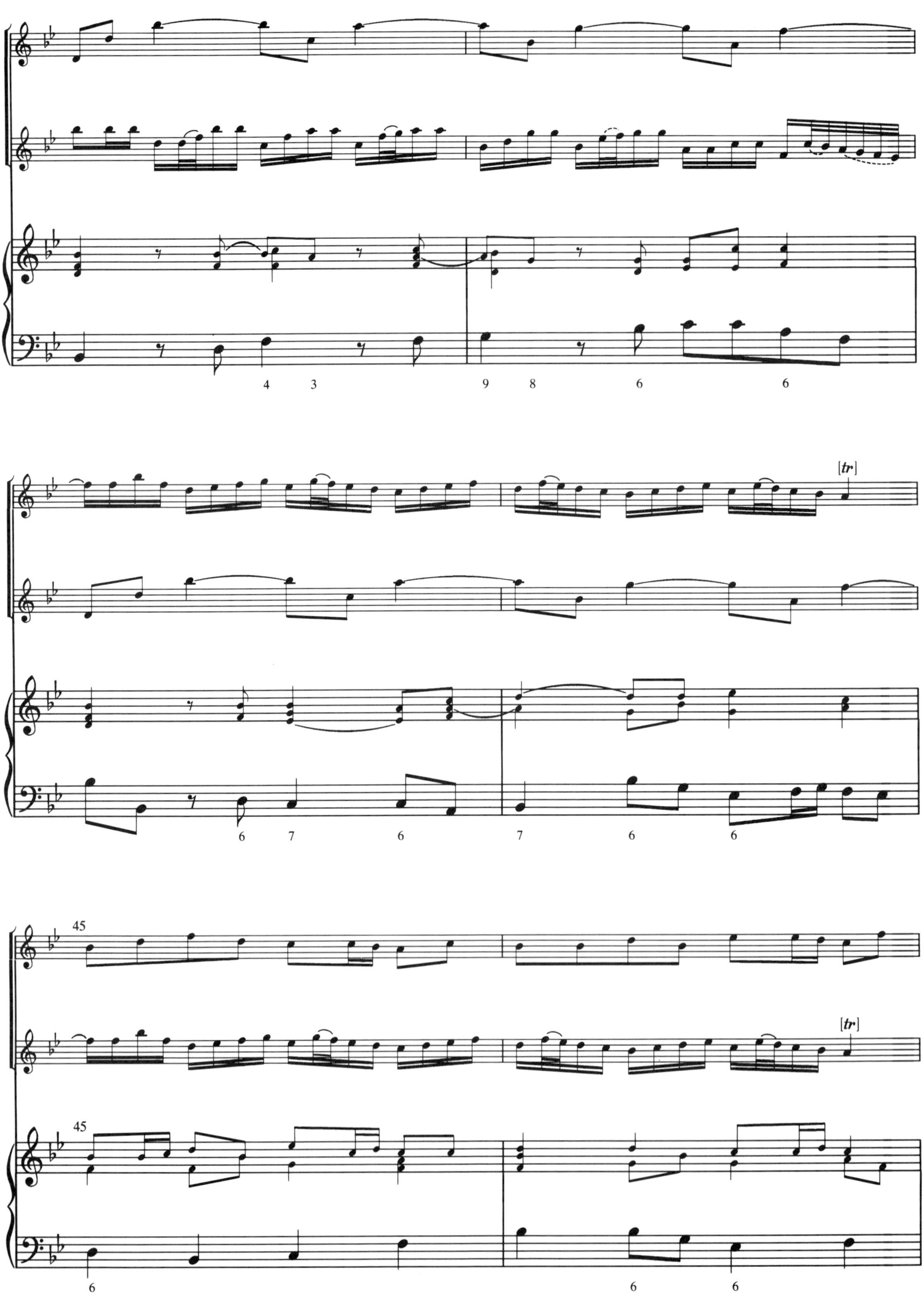
4 3
9 8 6 6
[tr]
6 7 6
7 6 6
45
45
[tr]
6
6 6

7

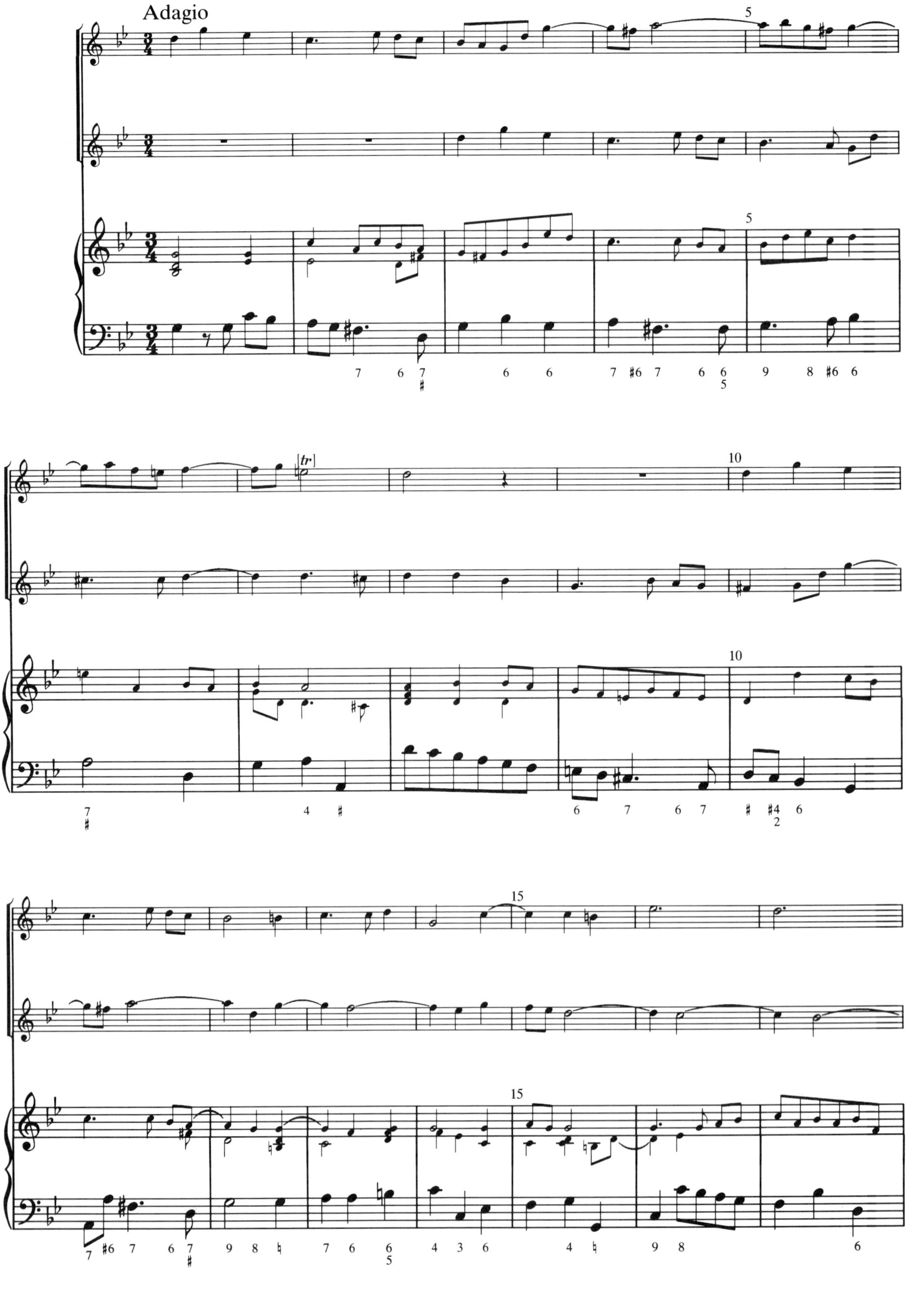
Adagio
5
5
[tr]
10
10
15
15

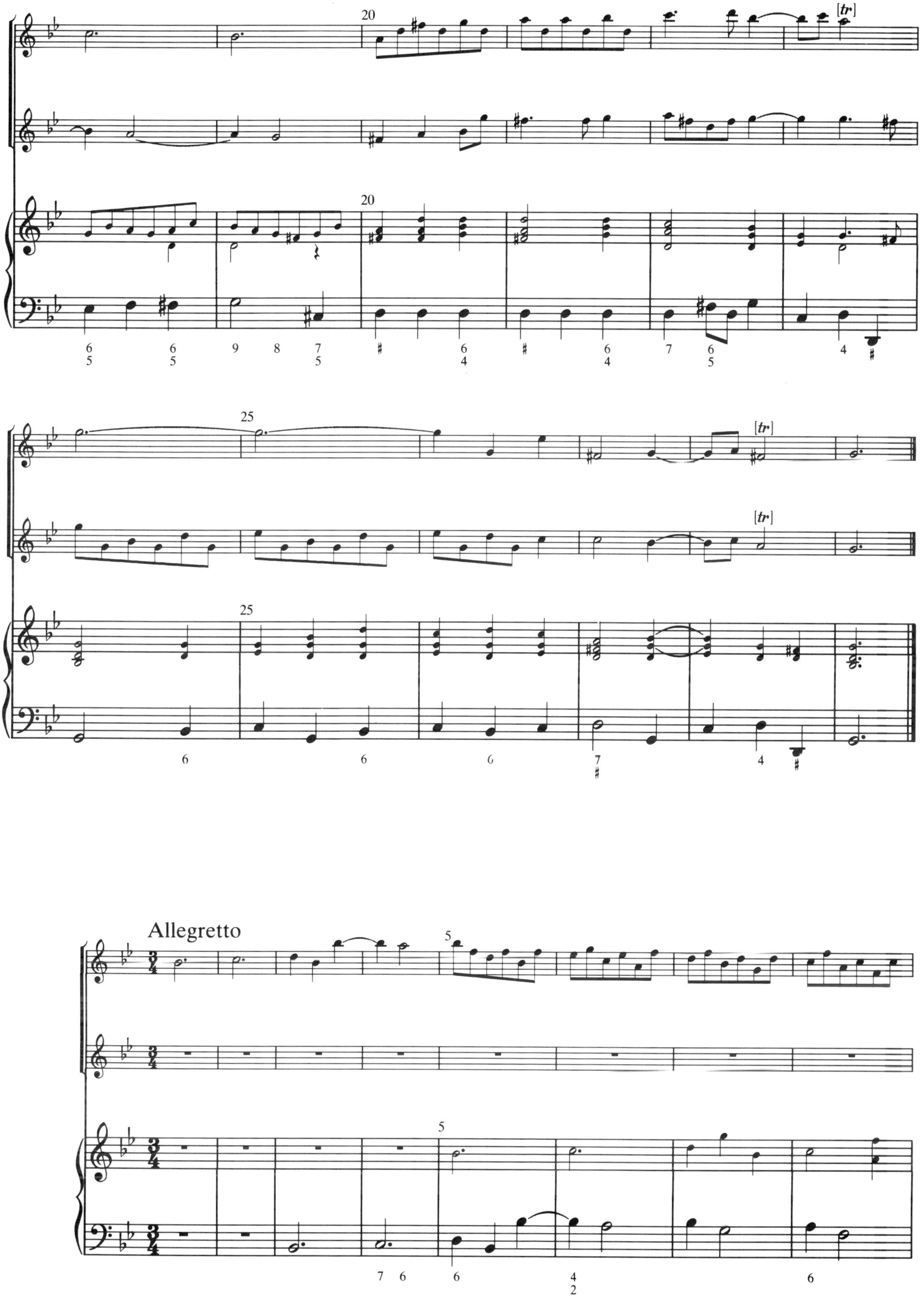
20
[tr]
25
Allegretto
5

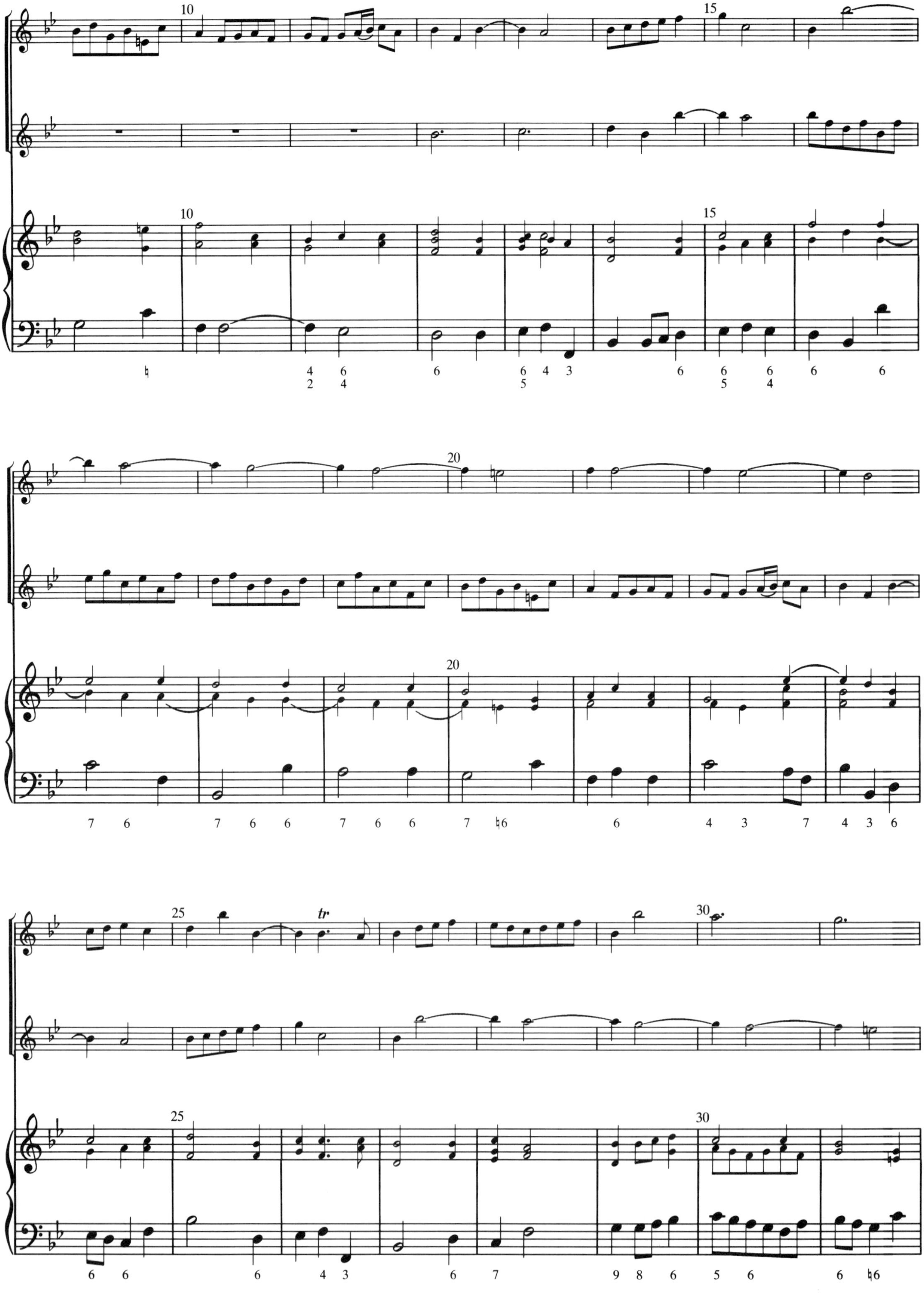

11

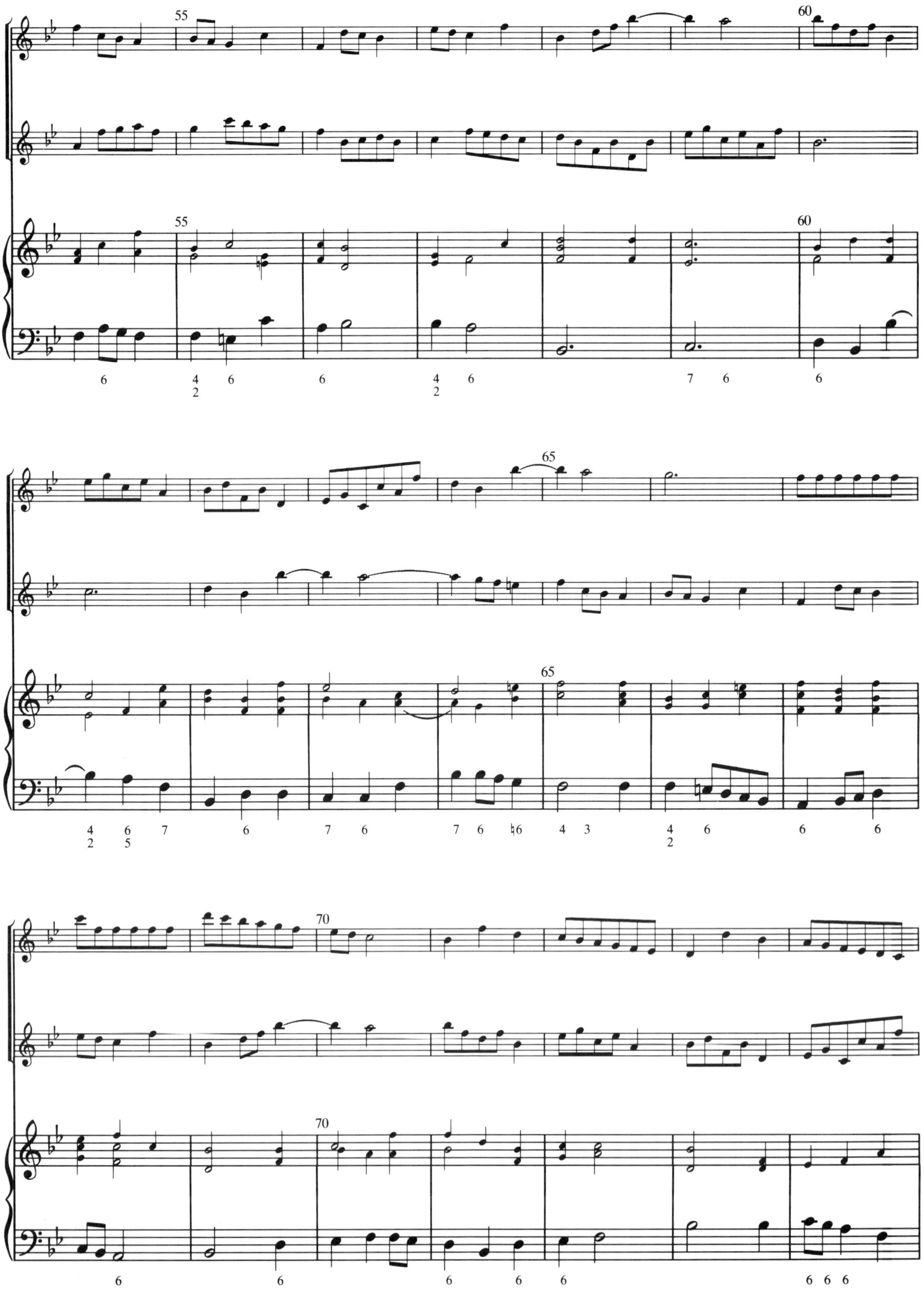
55
60
55
60
65
65
70
70

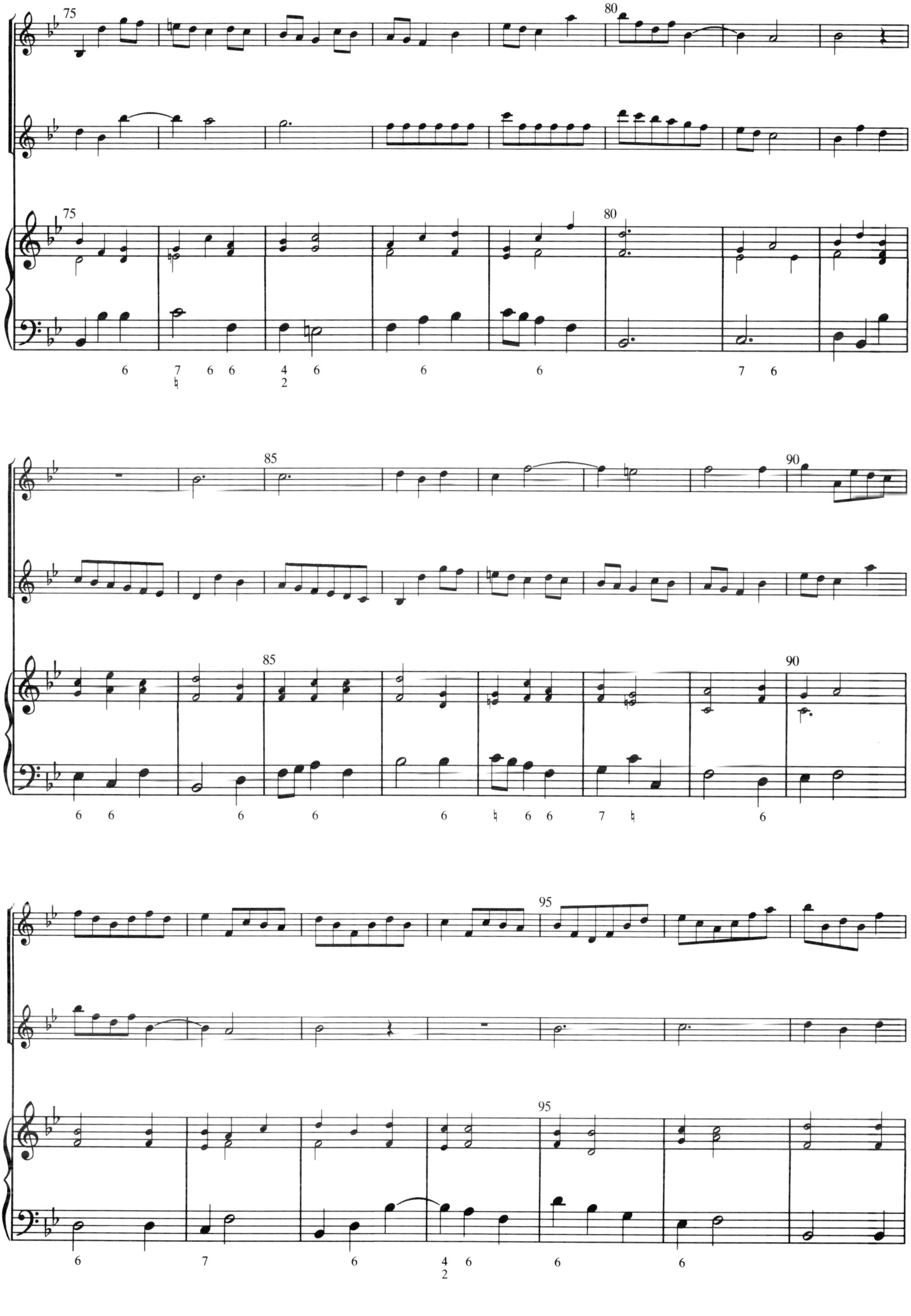

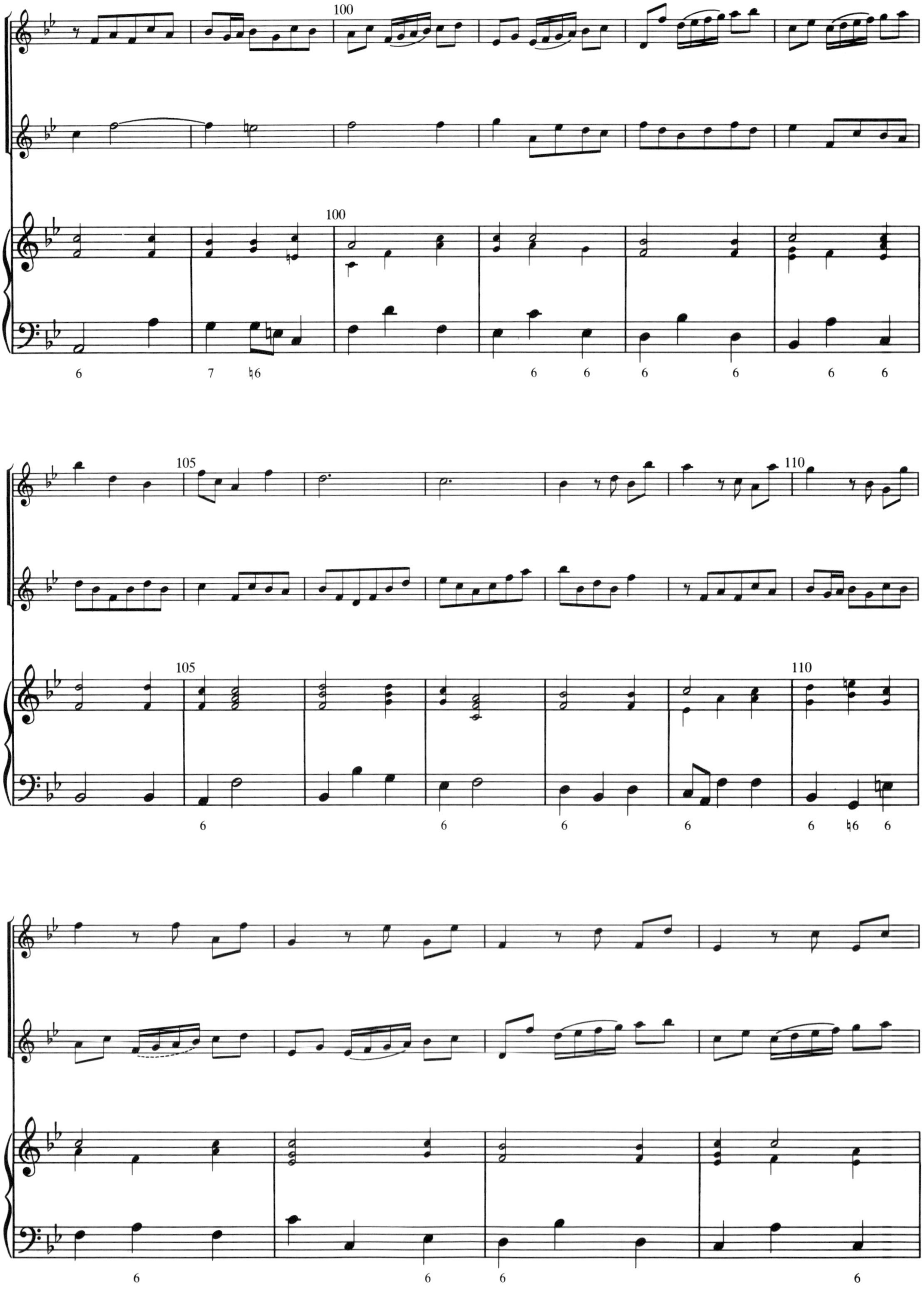
100
100
105
105
110
110

15

16

17

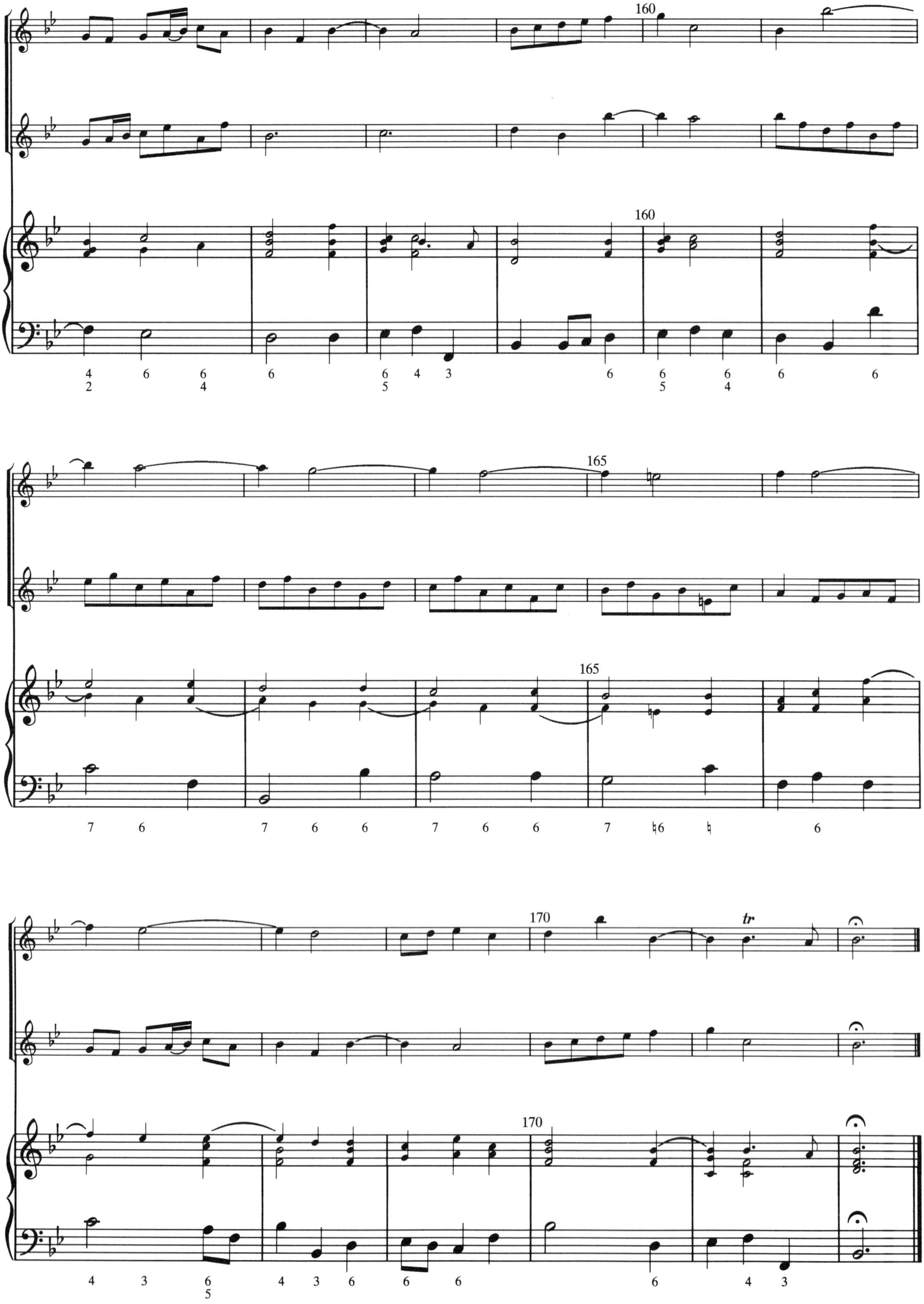
160
160
165
165
170
tr
170

Suite I

ALLEMANDA
Larghetto

20

21

22

GIGA
Allegro

24

25

SARABANDA
Allegro

27

28

Sonata II

Grave. Adagio

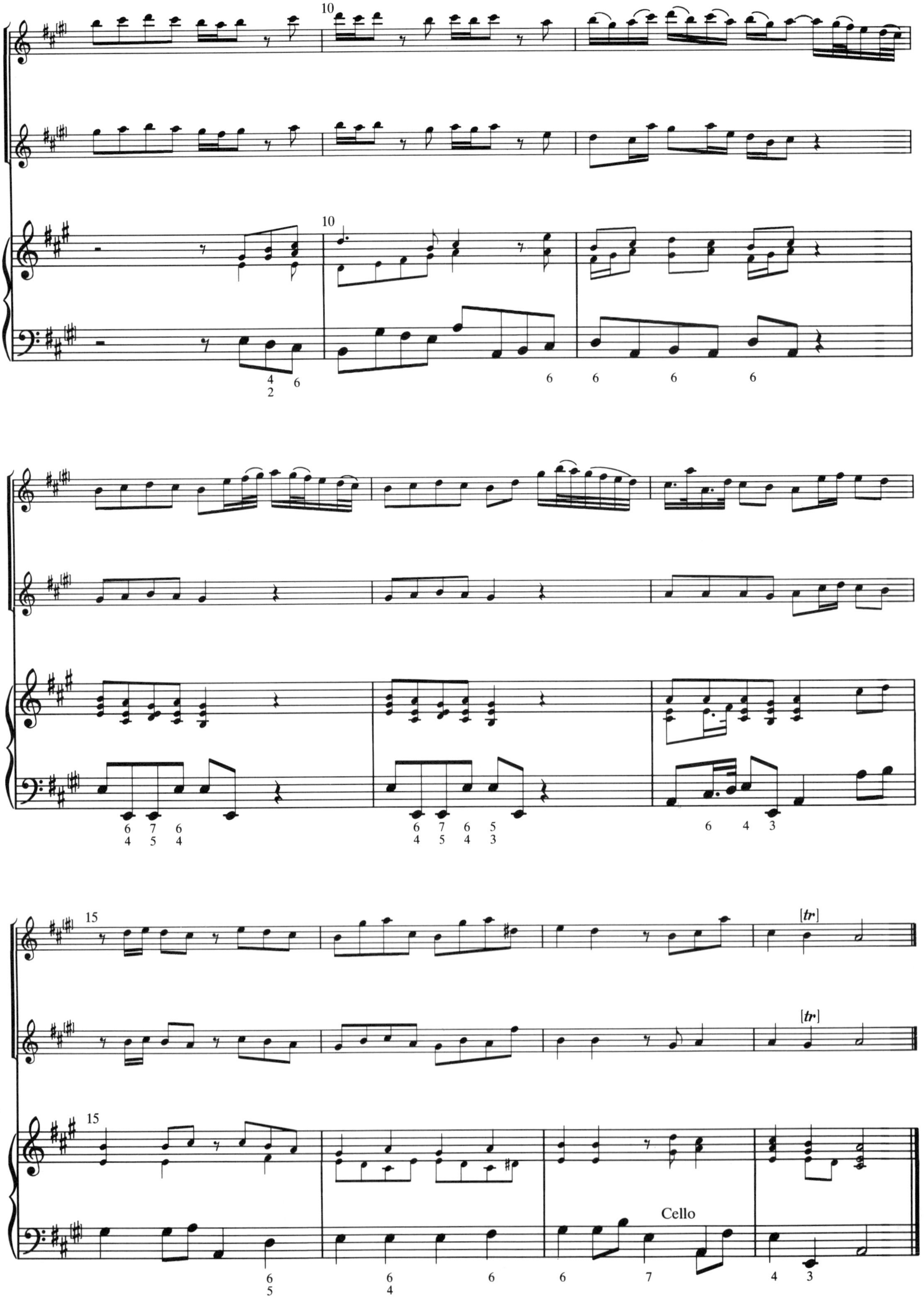
10
15
[tr]
Cello

31

32

33

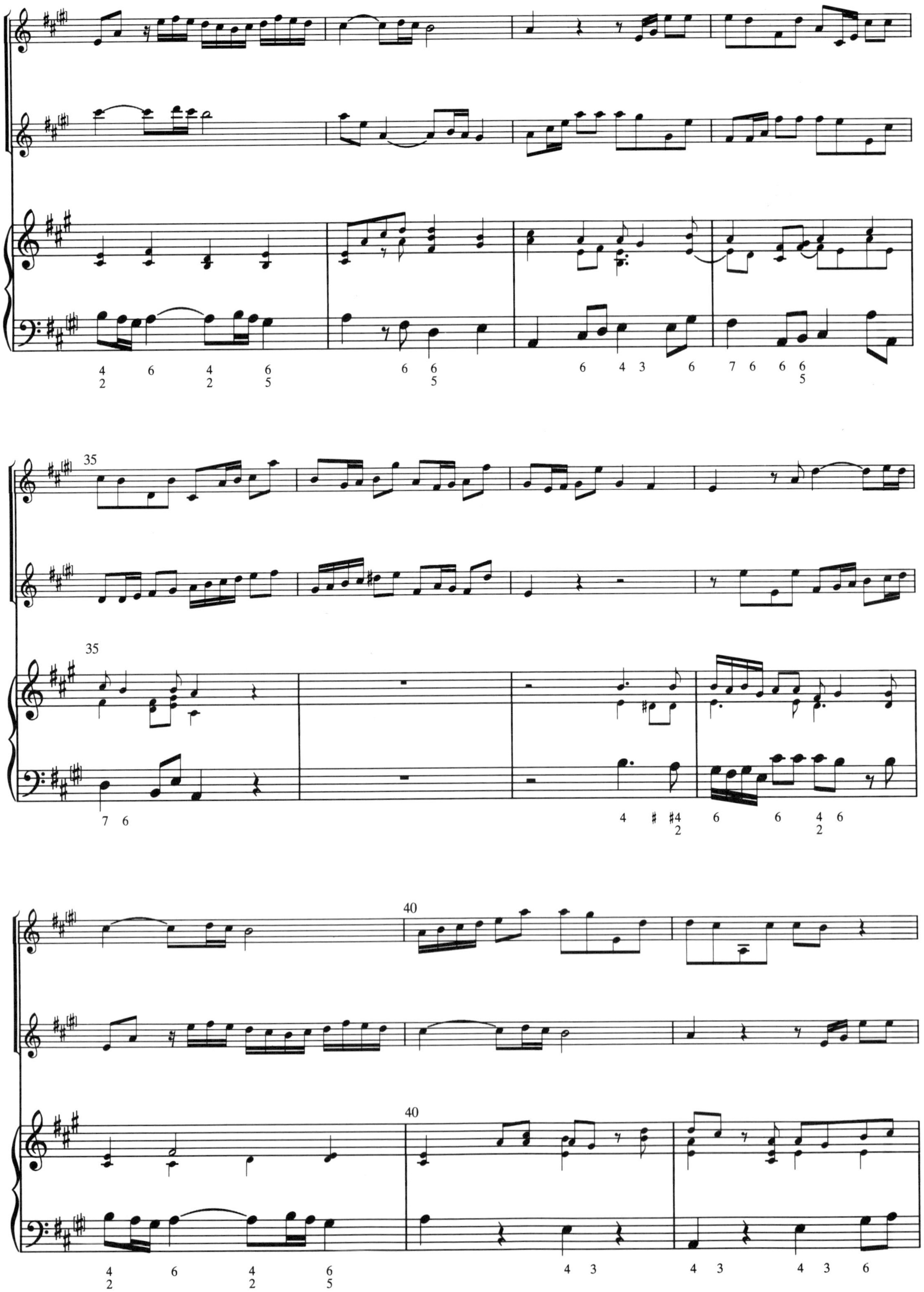
35
35
40
40

35

36

37

38

39

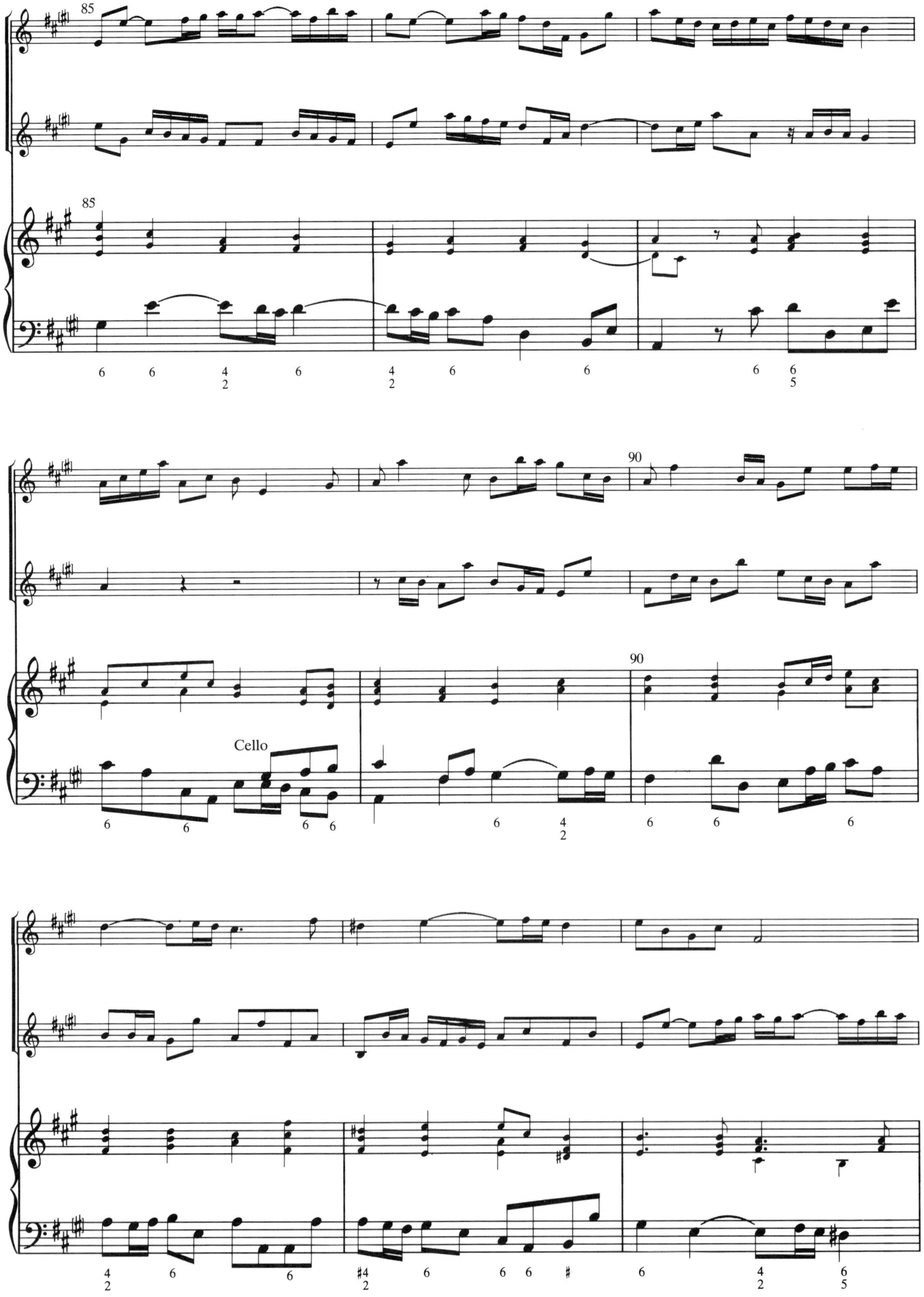
85
85
Cello
90
90

41

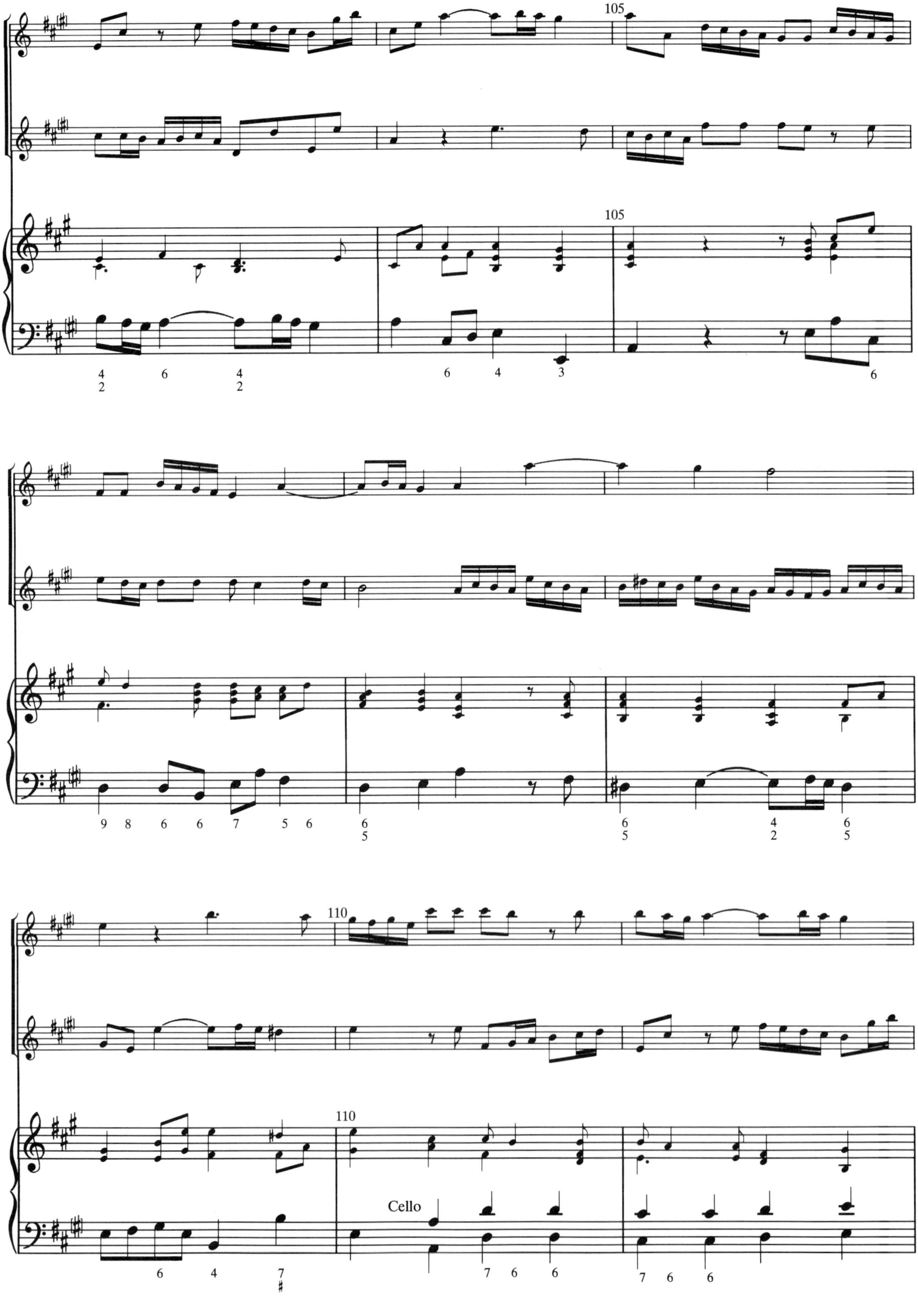
105
105
110
110
Cello

43

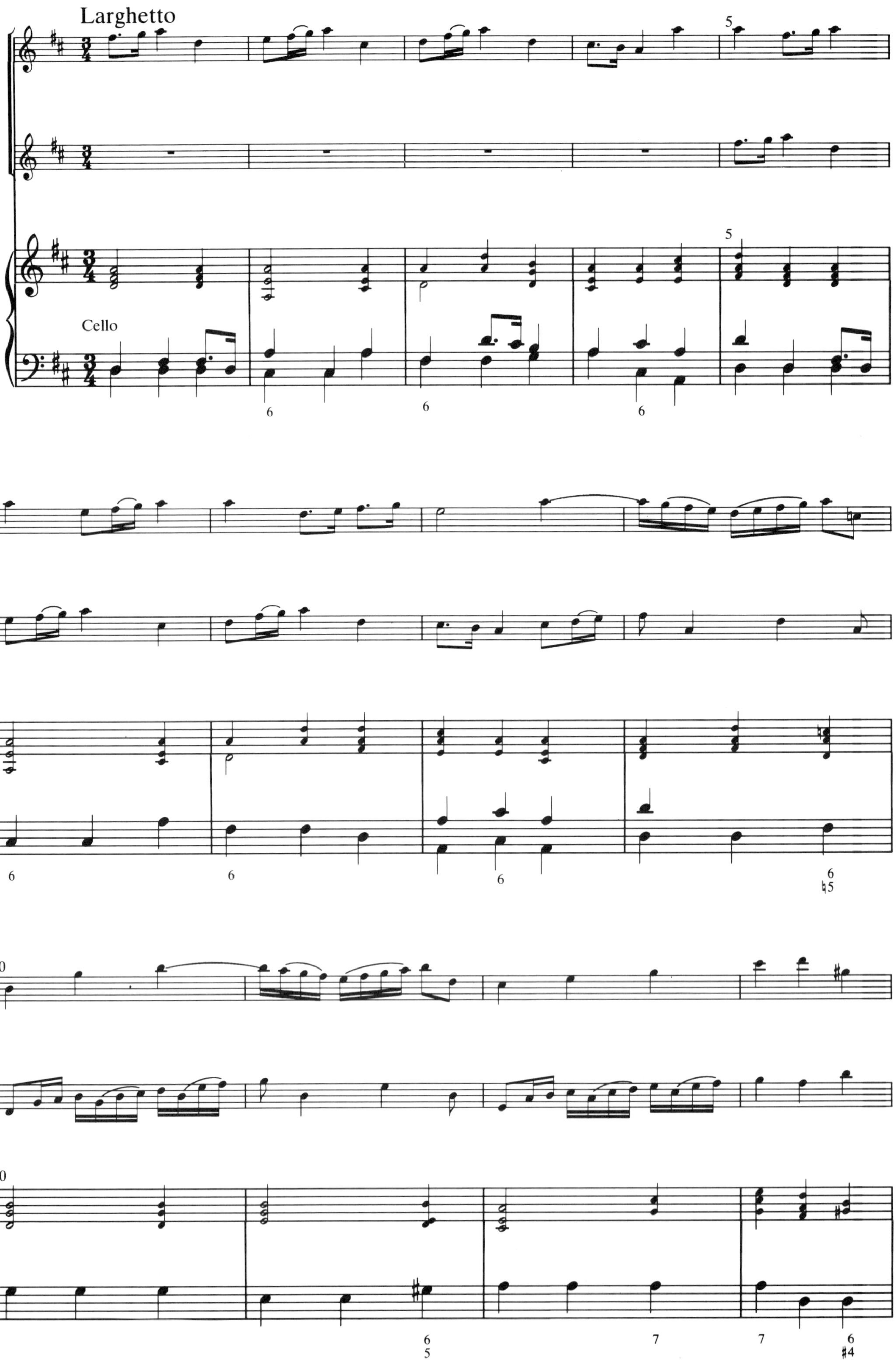
Larghetto
Cello

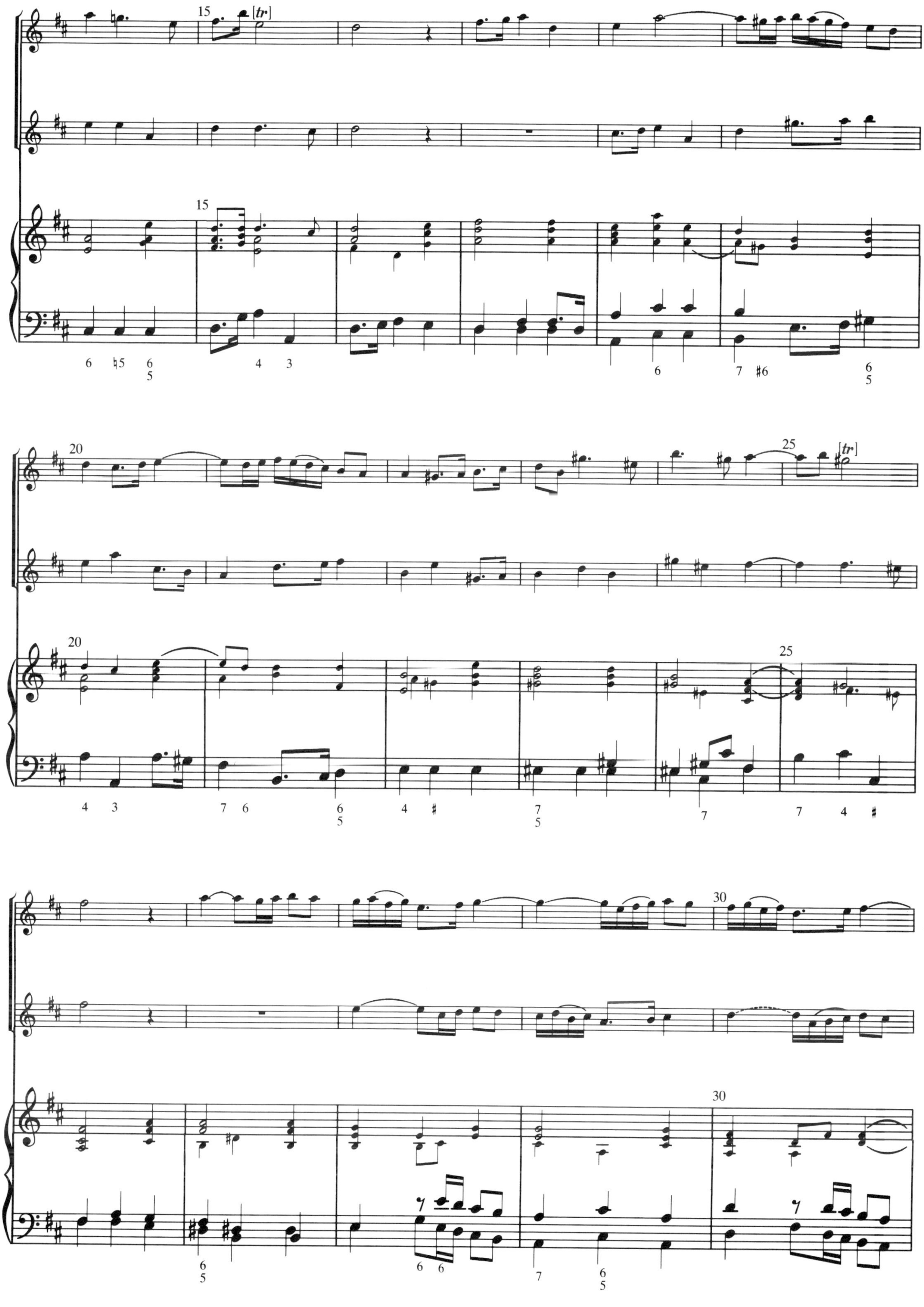

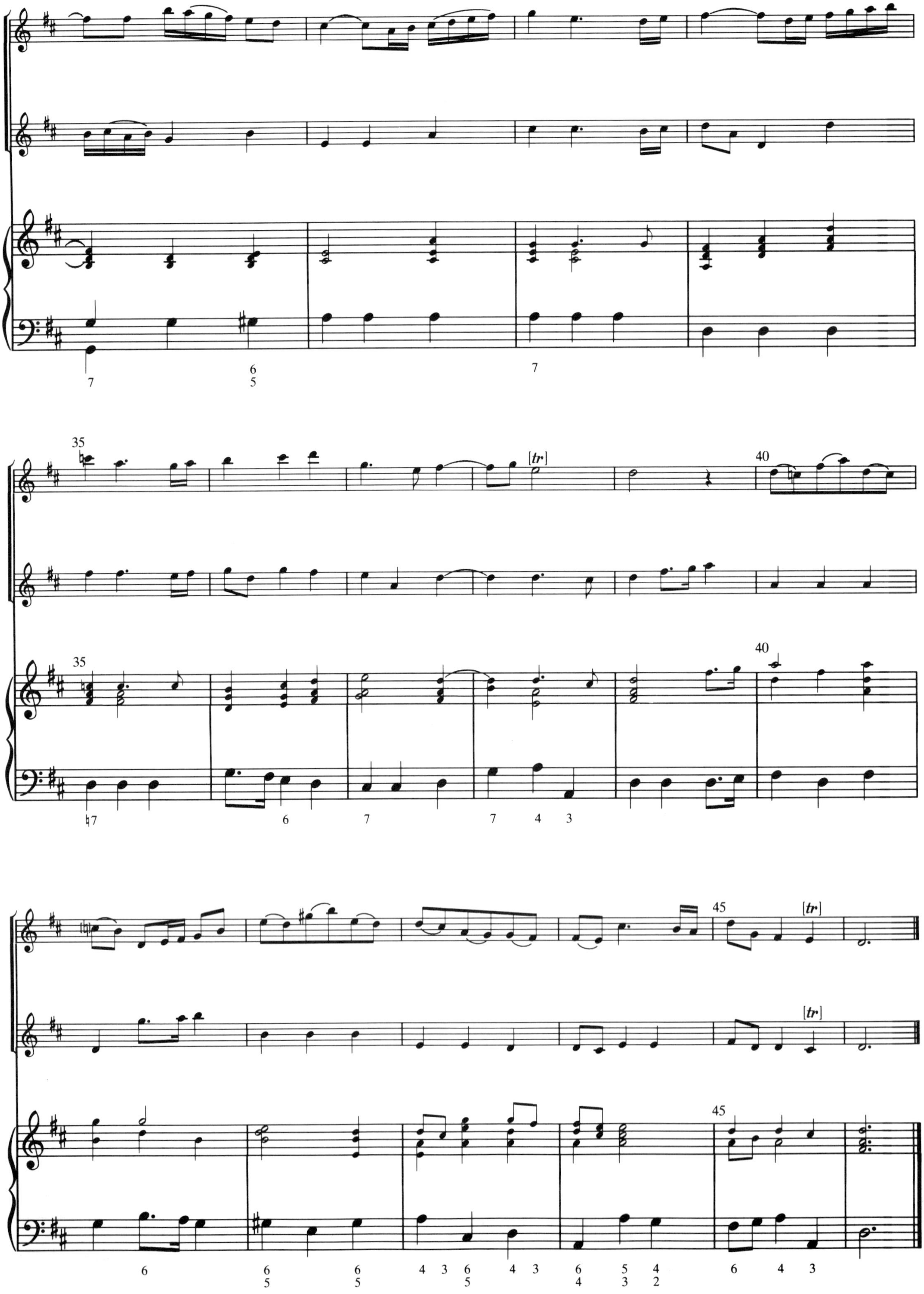
35
[tr]
40
35
40
[tr]
45
[tr]
45

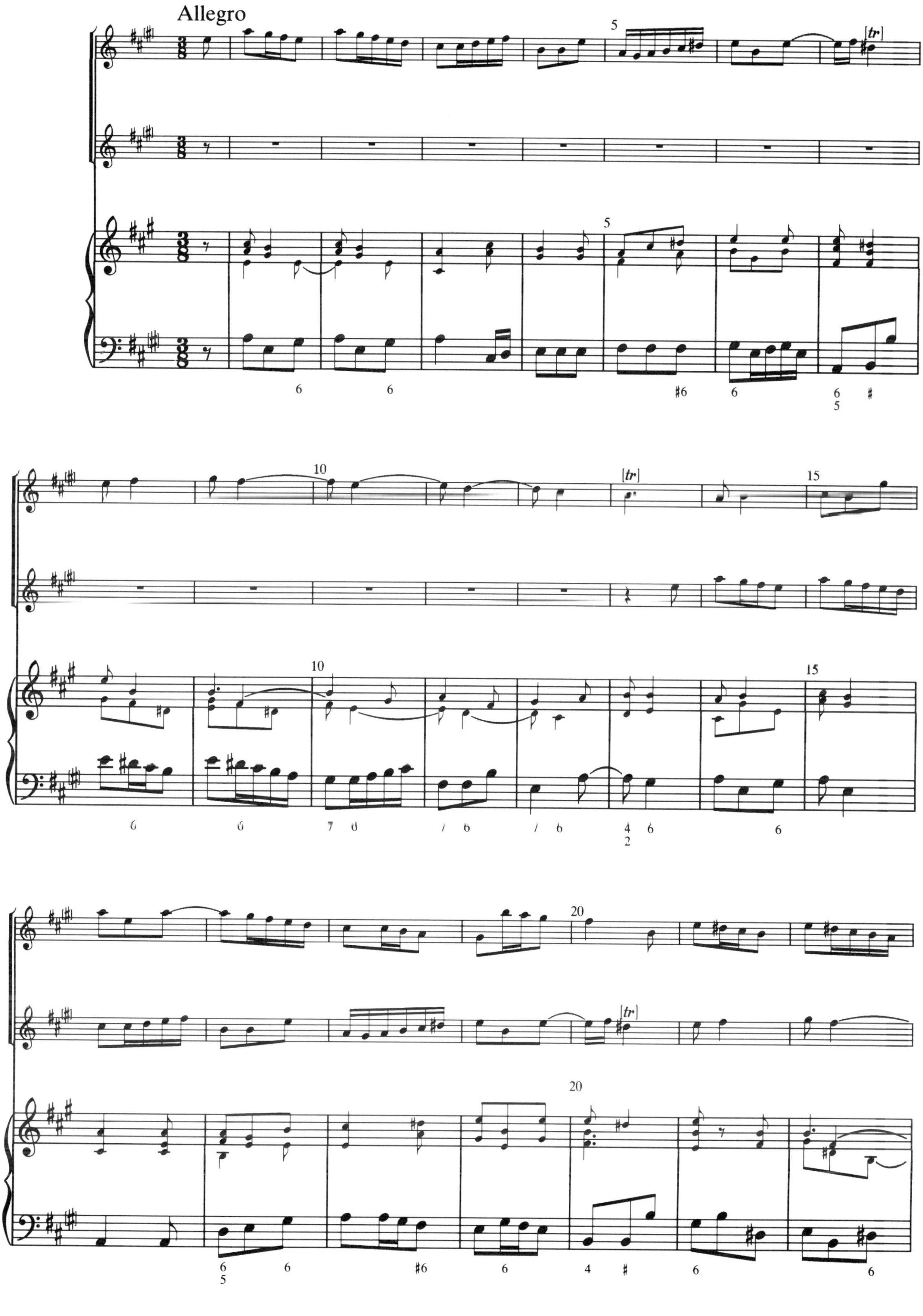
Allegro

48

49

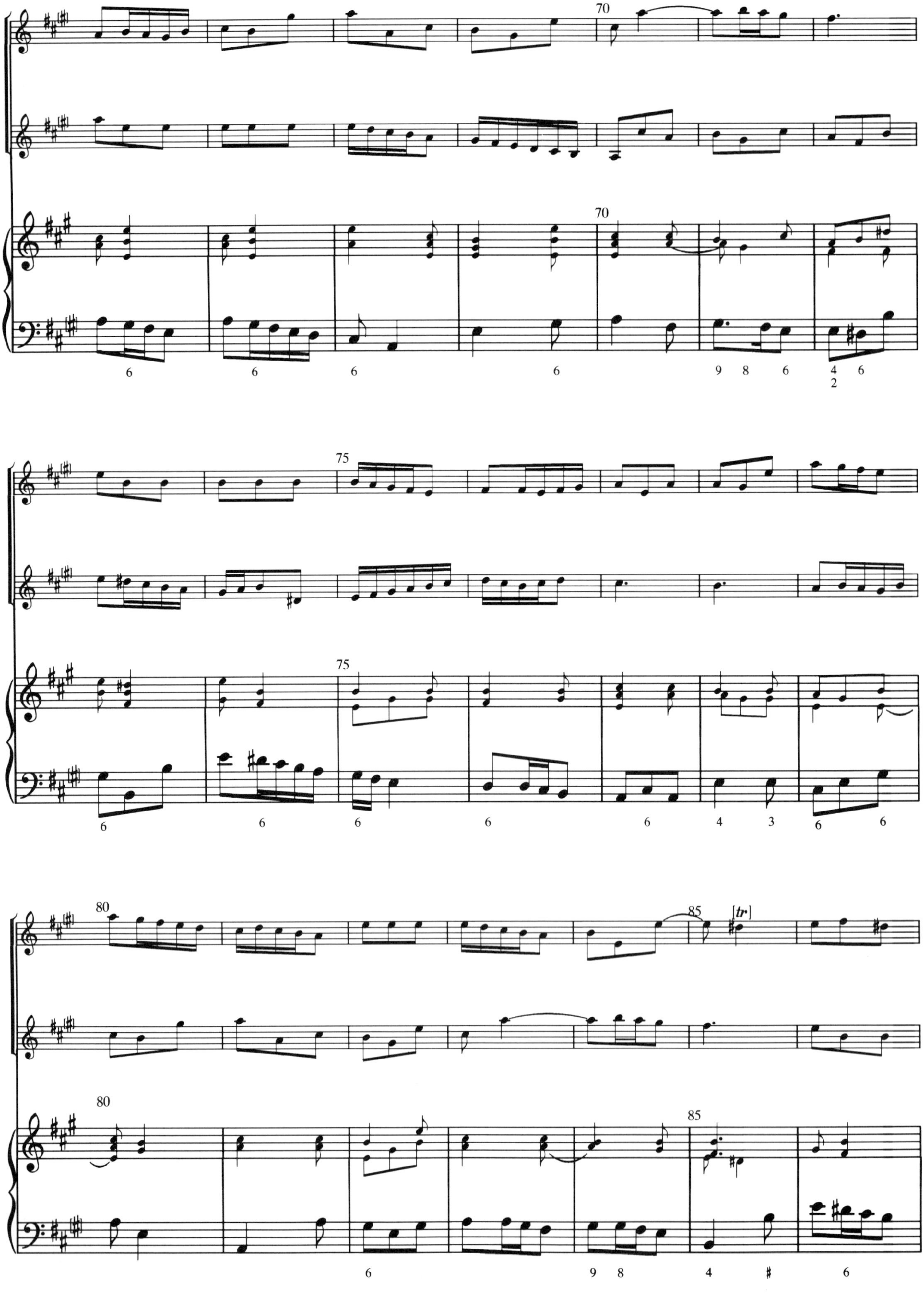
[tr]

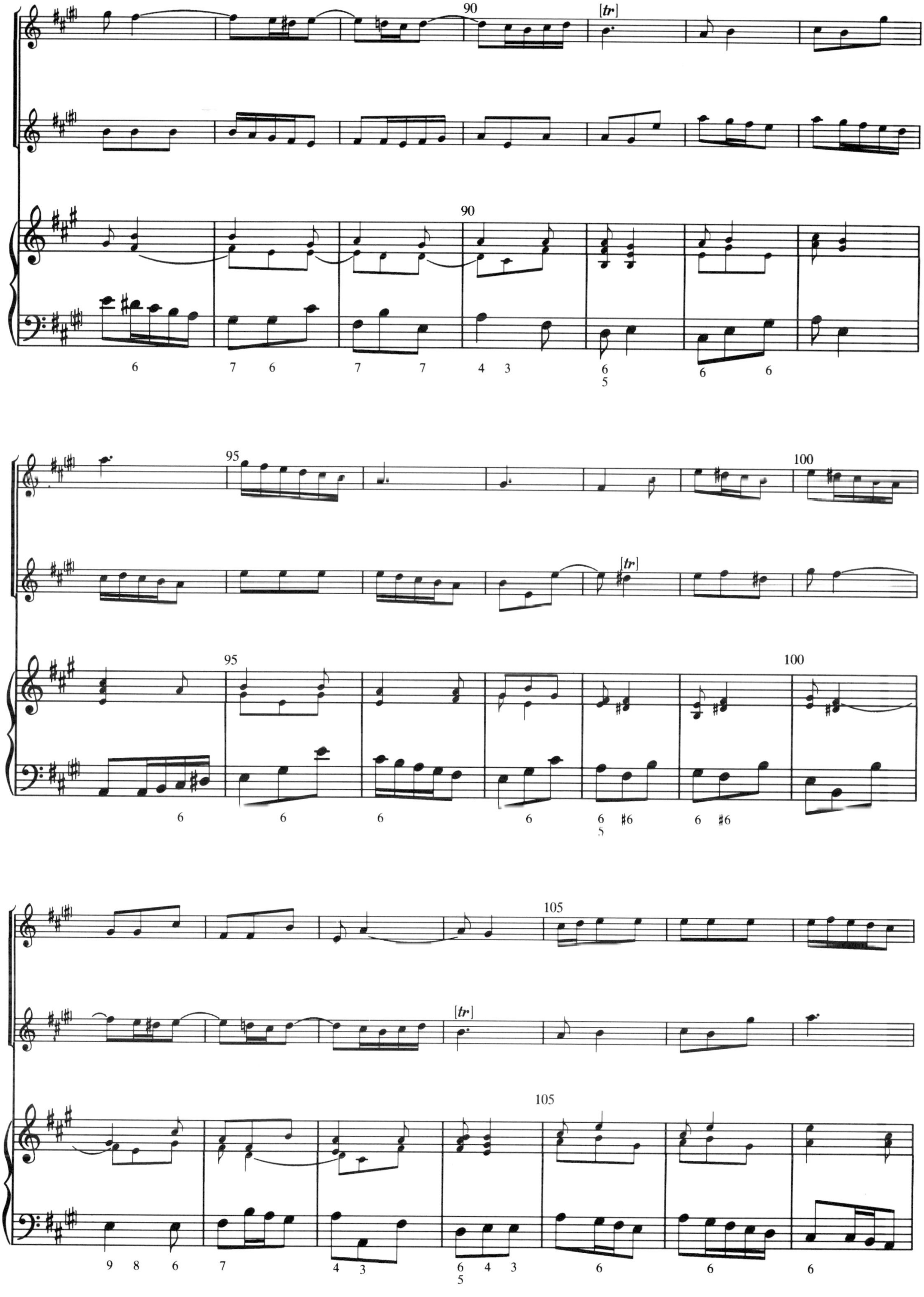
90
[tr]
95
100
[tr]
105

52

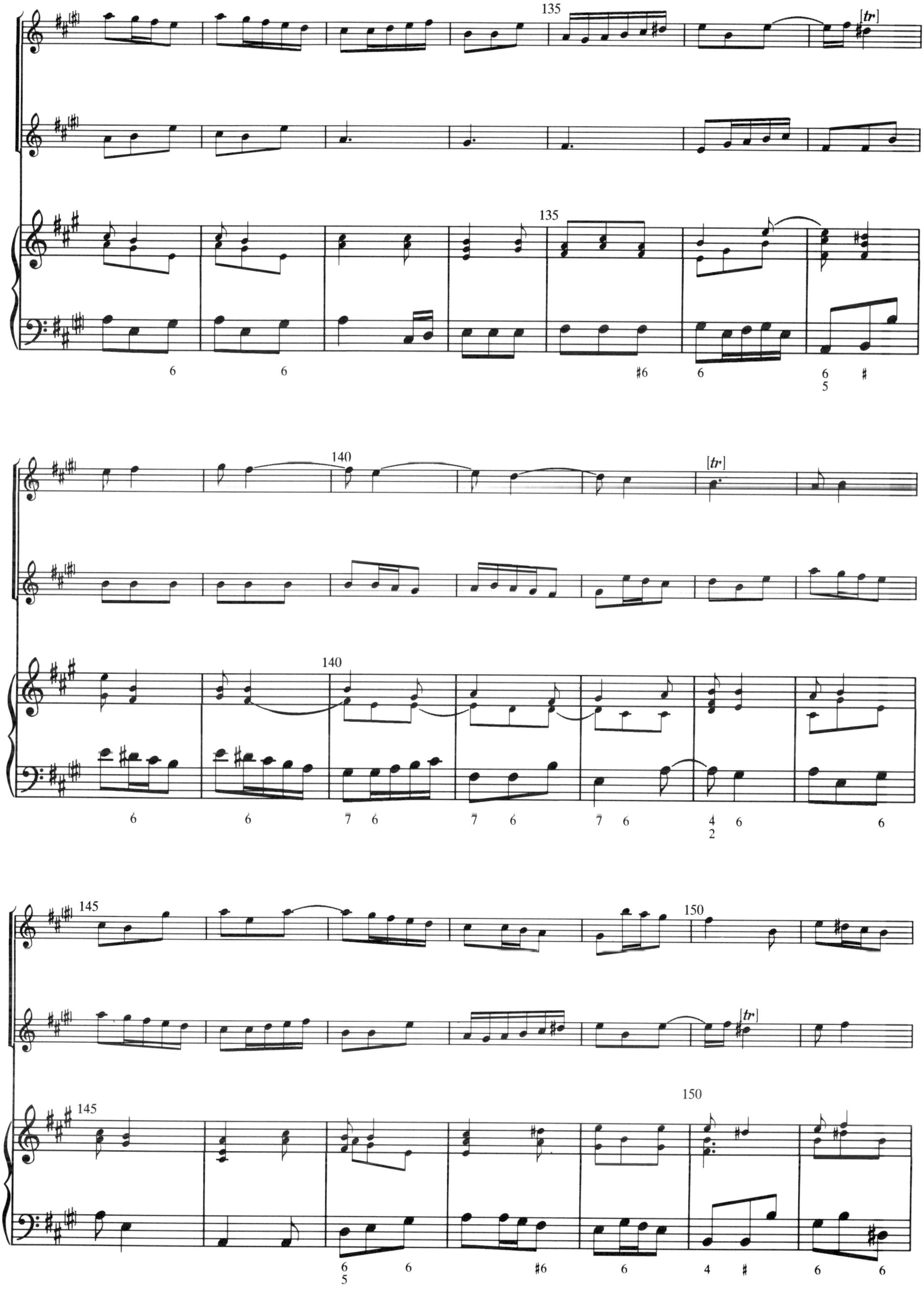
135
[tr]
140
[tr]
145
150
[tr]

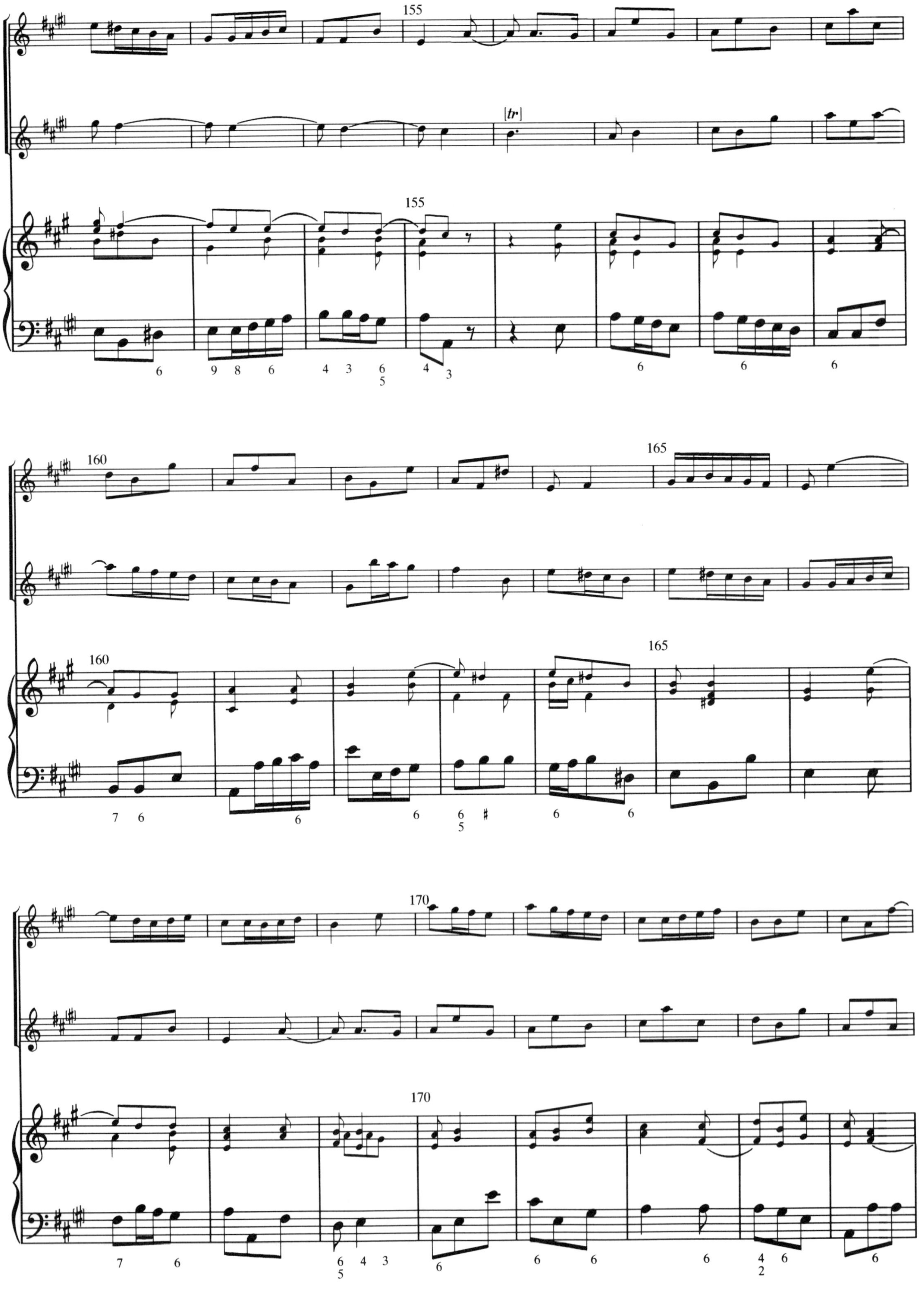
155
[tr]
160
165
170

55

Suite II

ALLEMANDA
Allegro

57

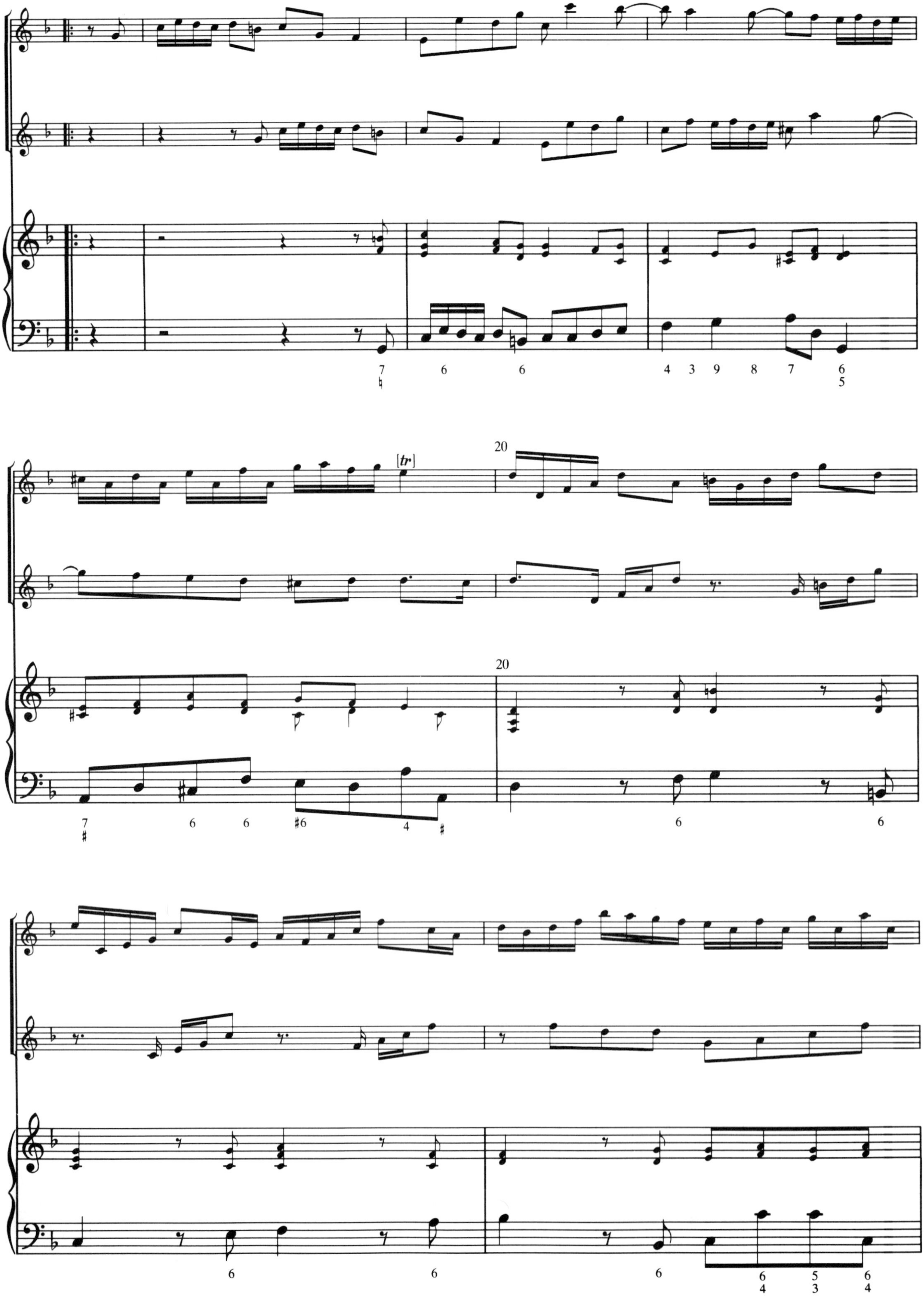
20
[tr]

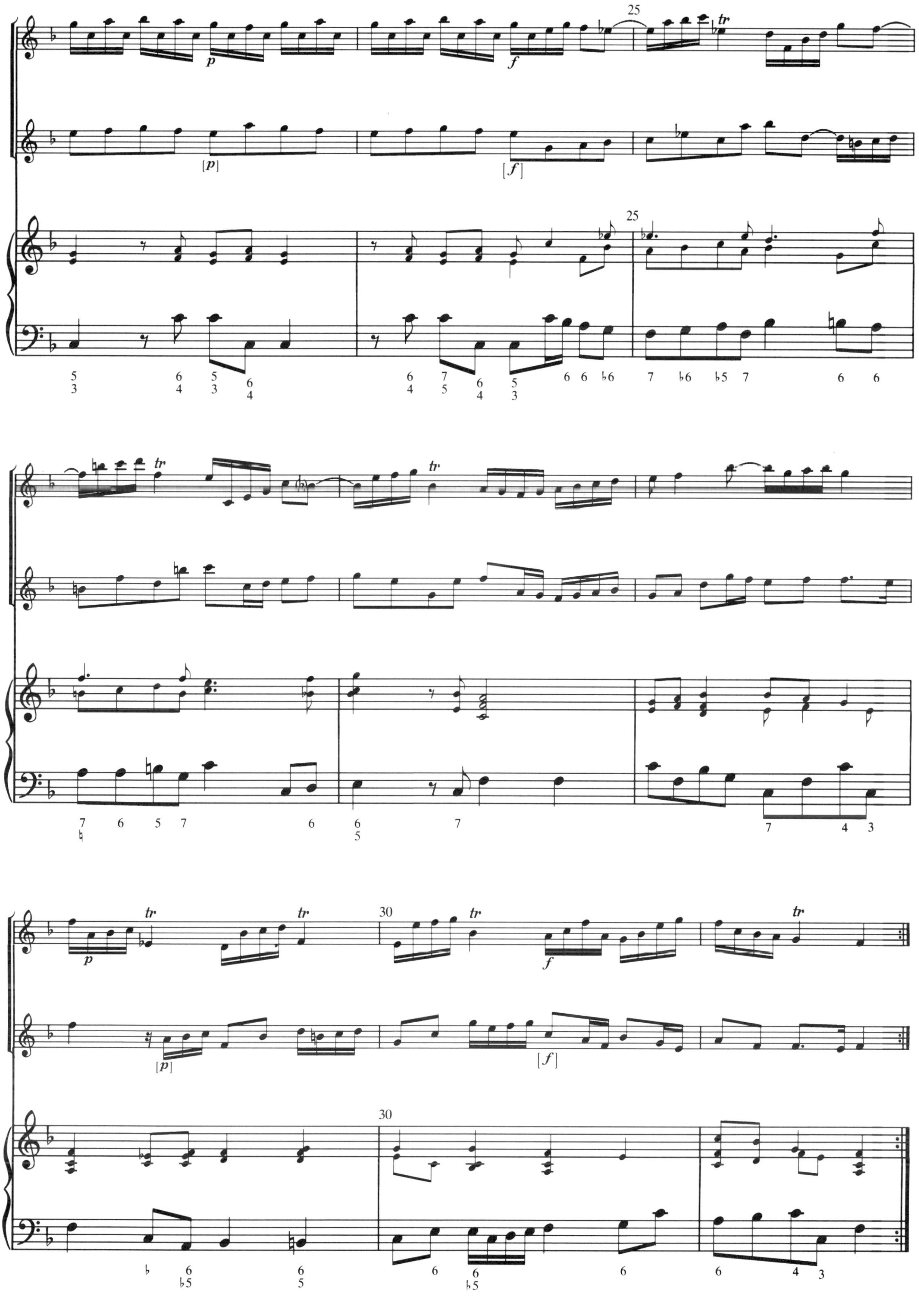
25
tr
p
f
[p]
[f]
30

CORRENTE
Allegro

61

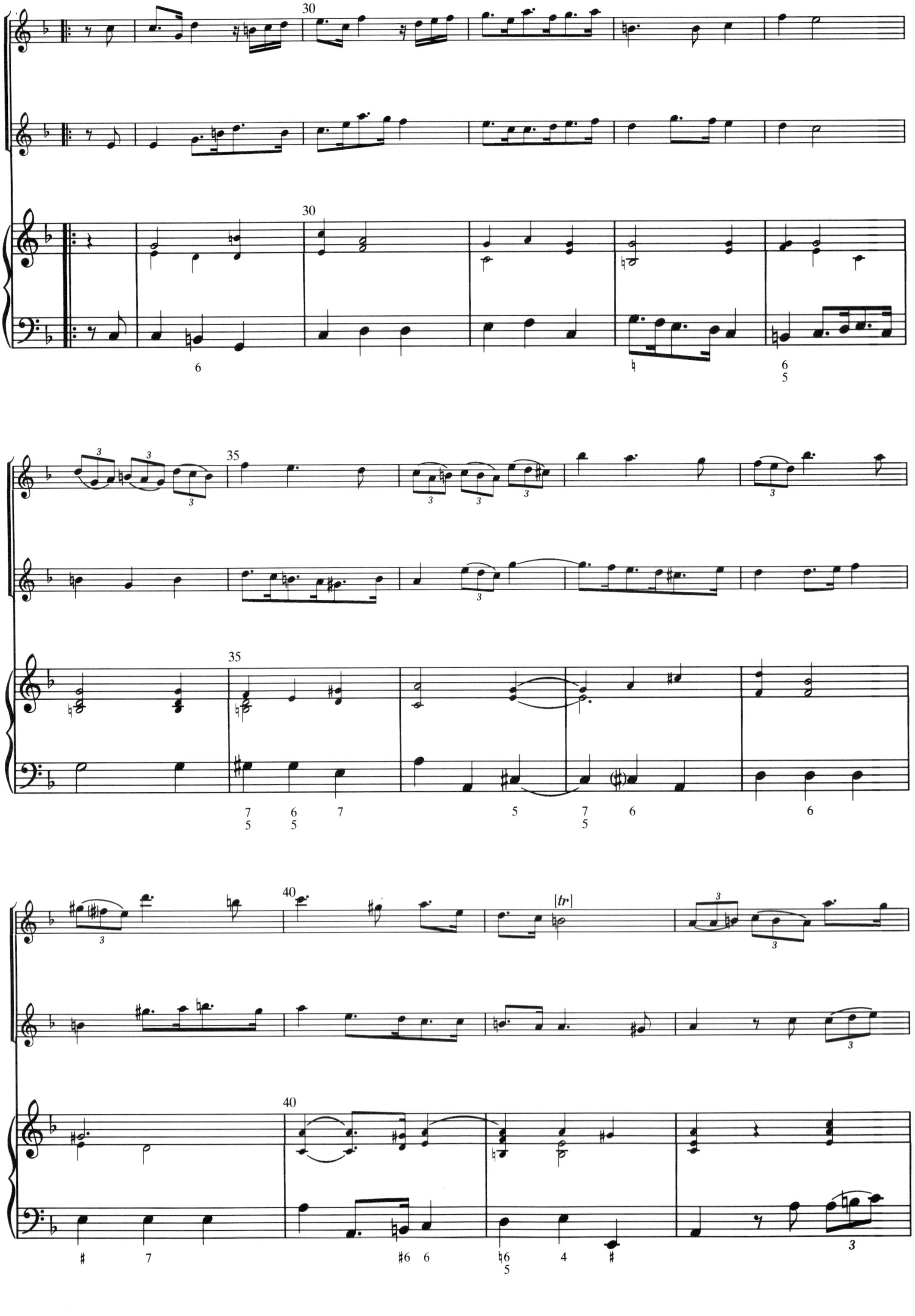

63

GAVOTTA
Allegro

65

Sonata III

67

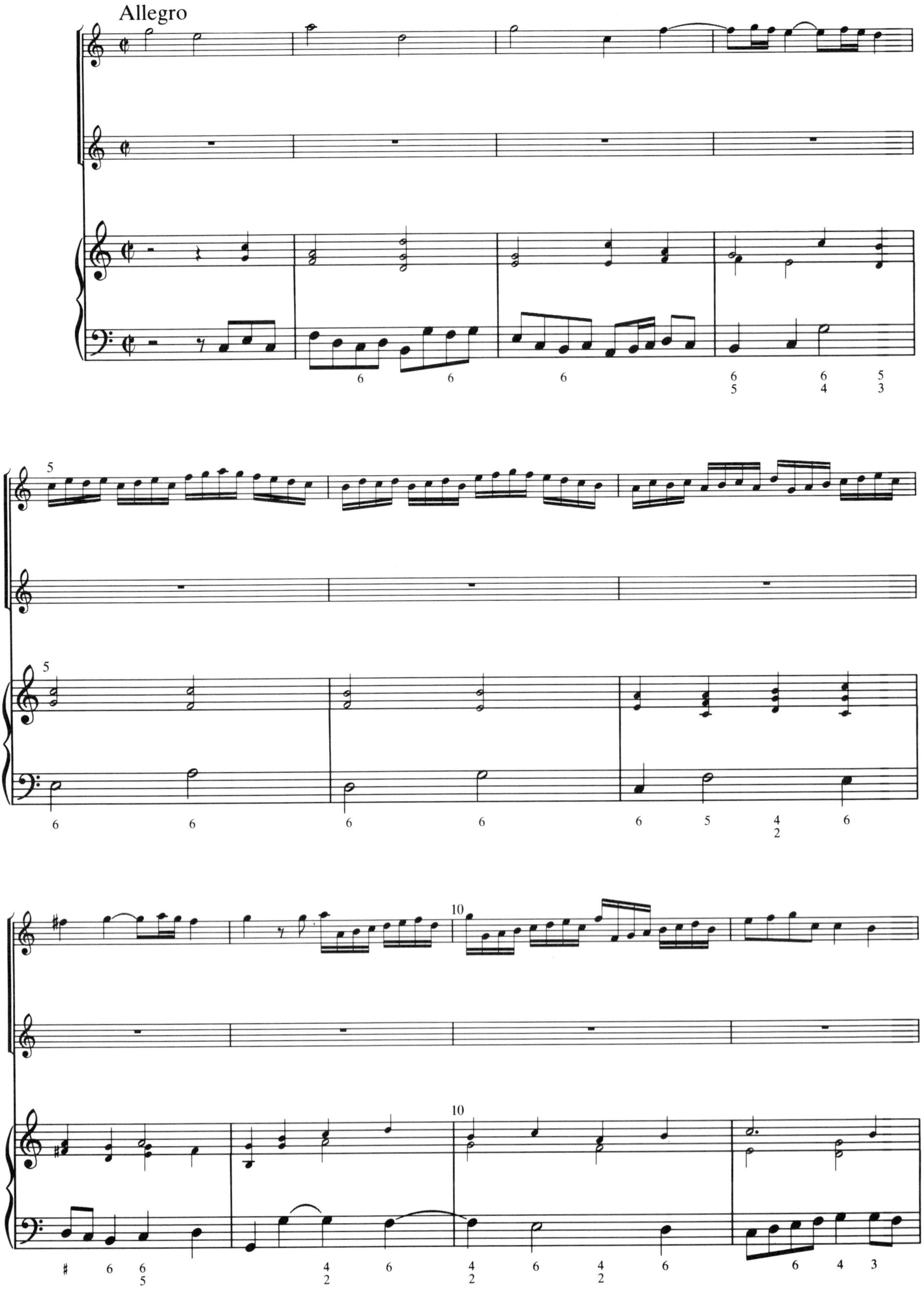
Allegro

69

70

71

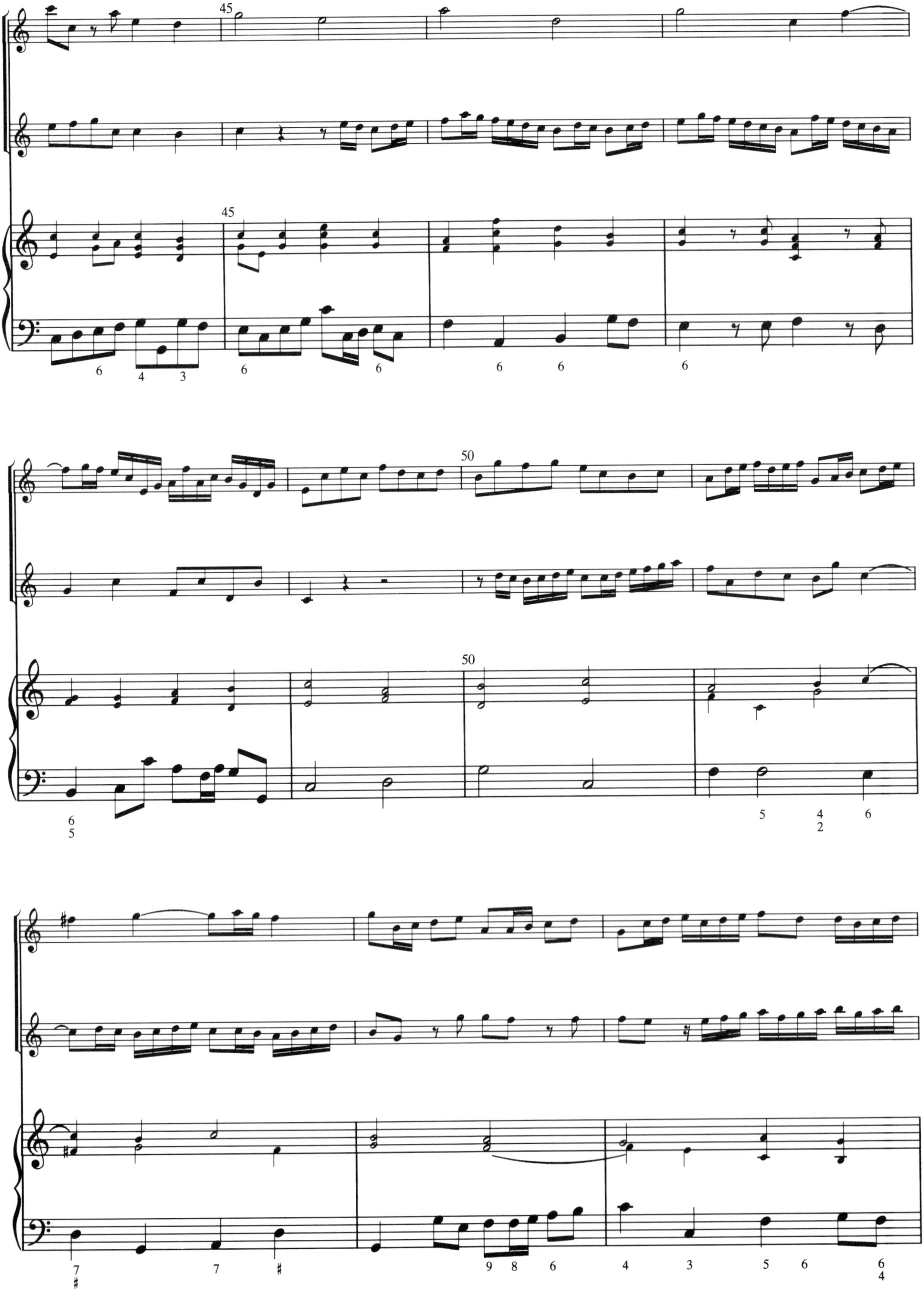

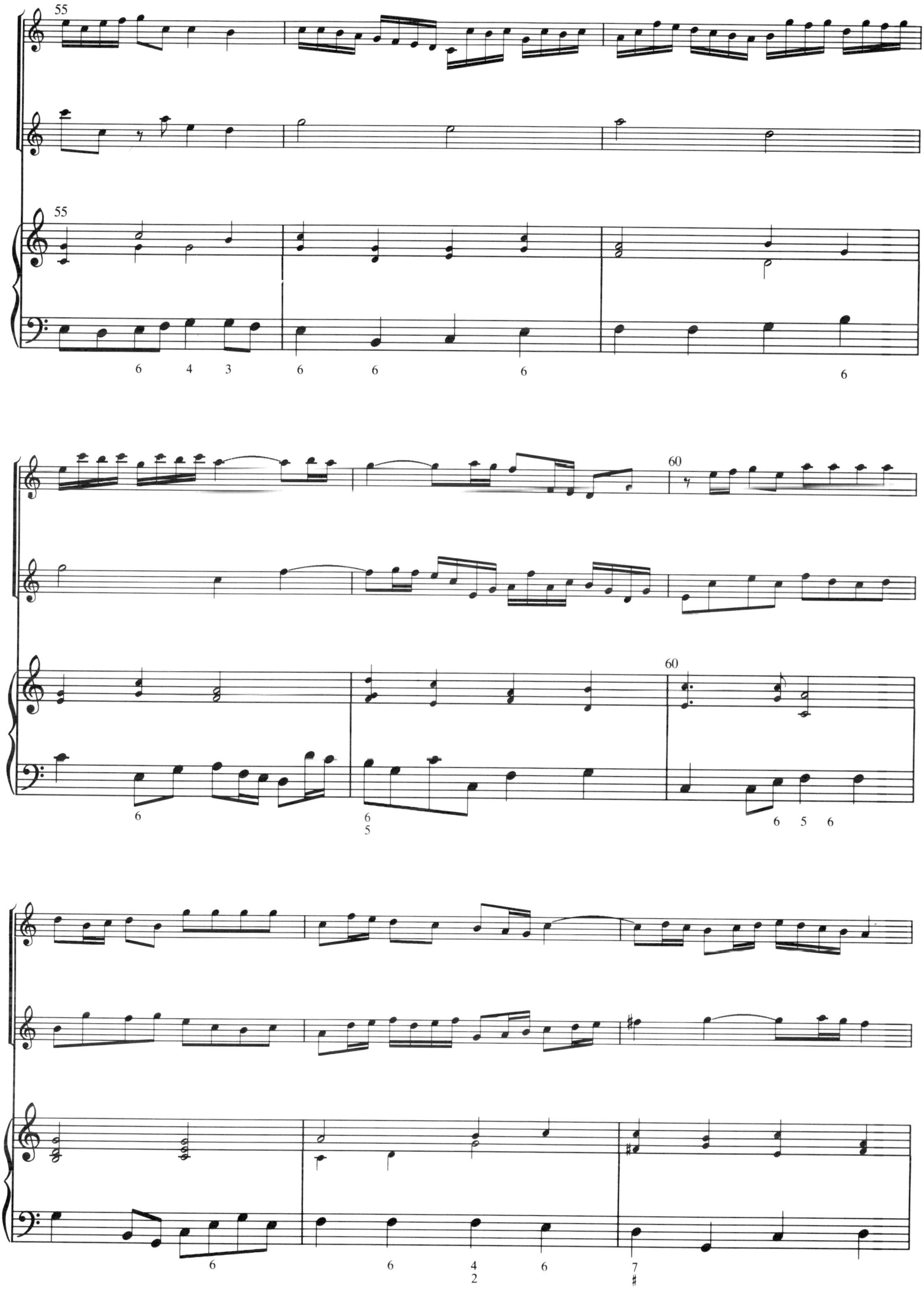
55
55
60
60

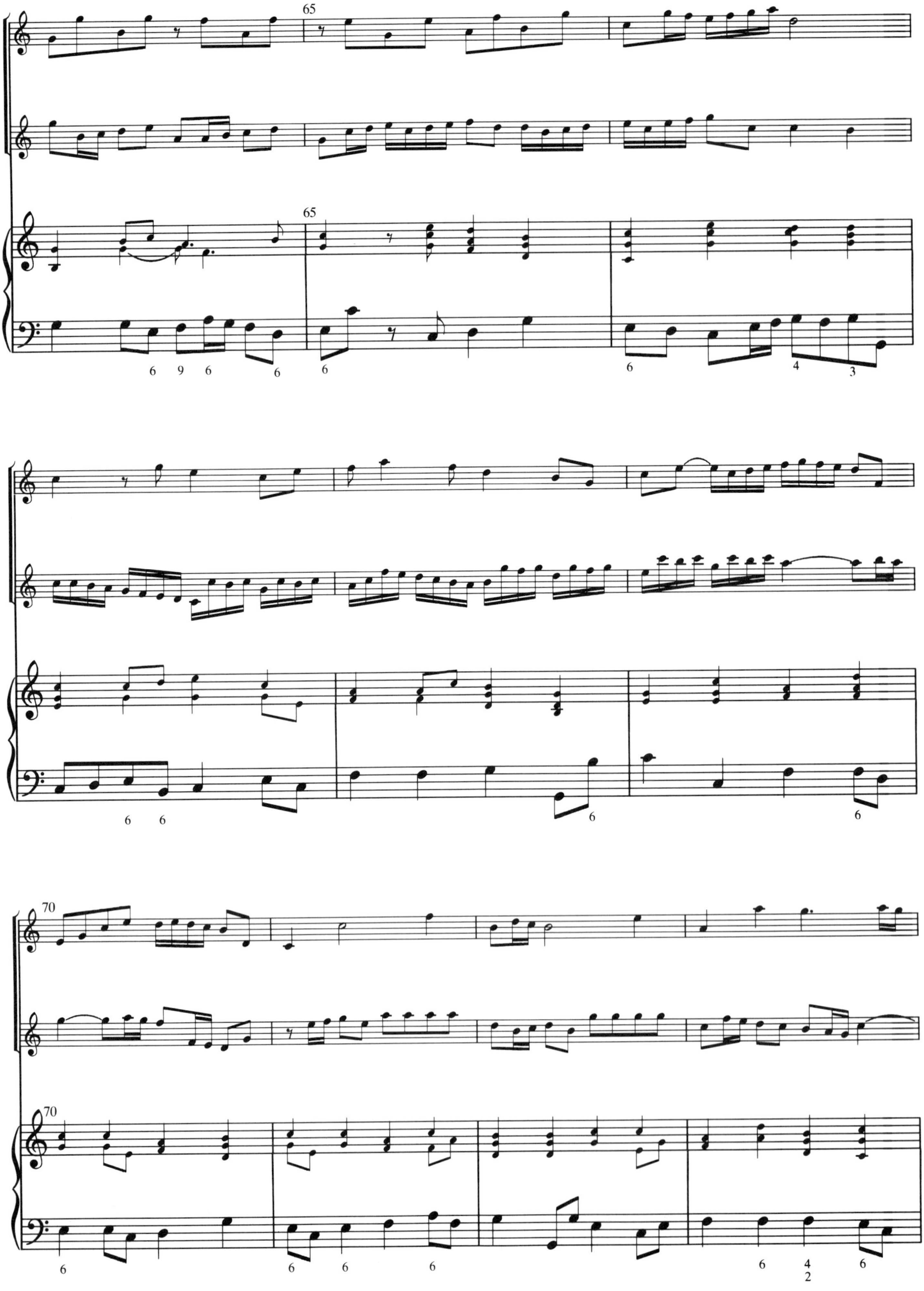
65
65
70
70

75

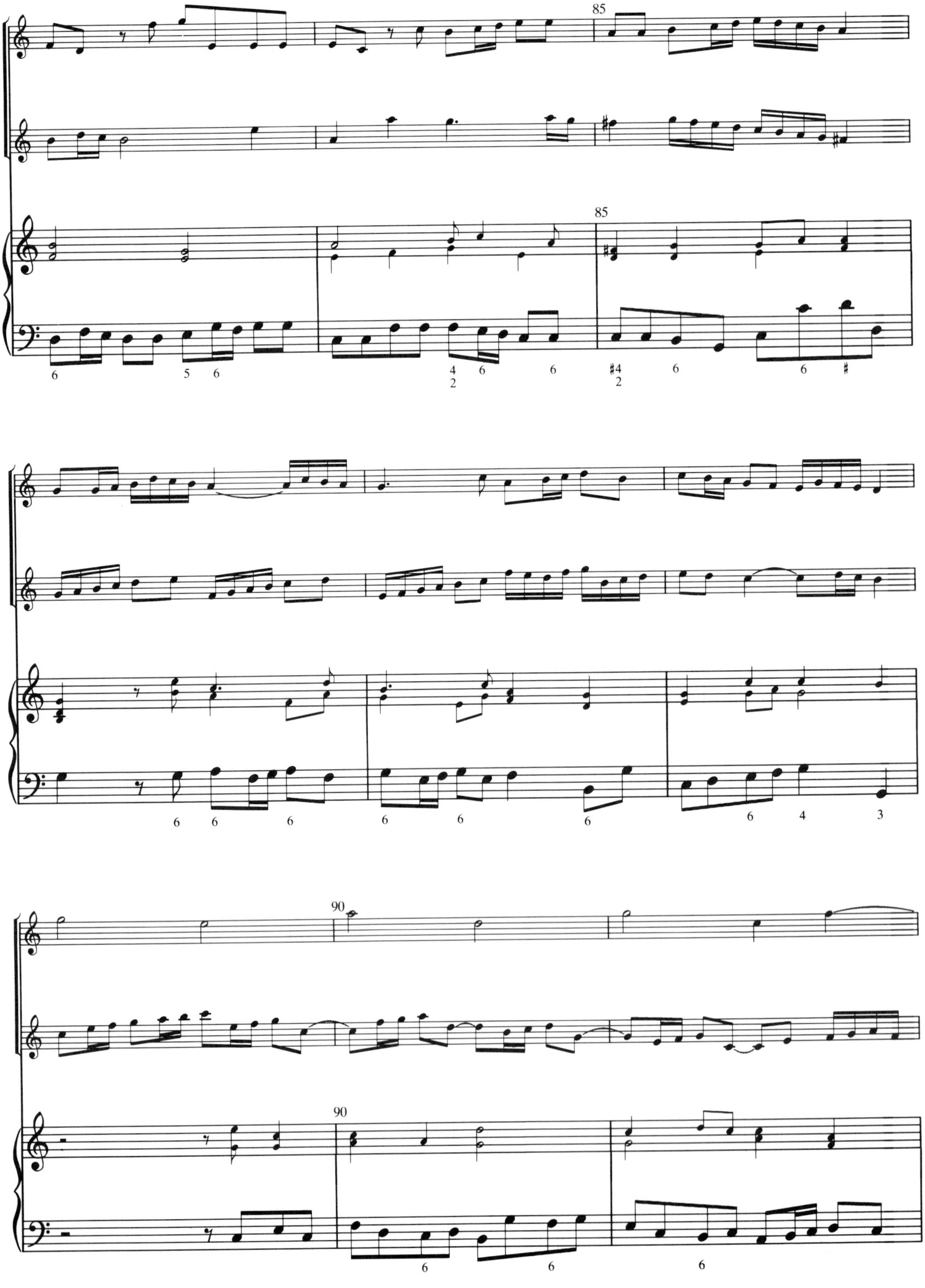
85
85
90
90

77

78

Larghetto

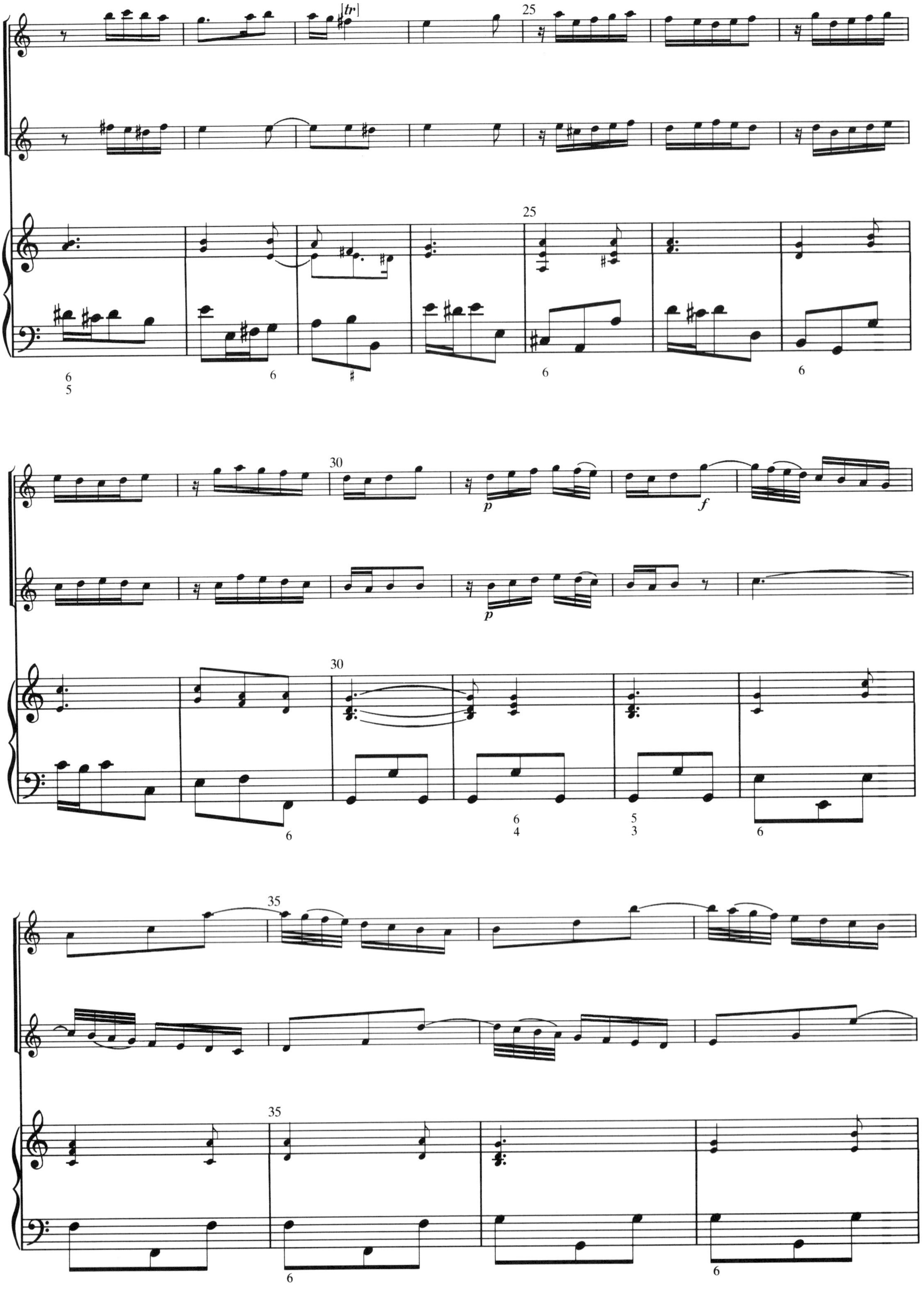
[tr]
25
30
p
f
35

81

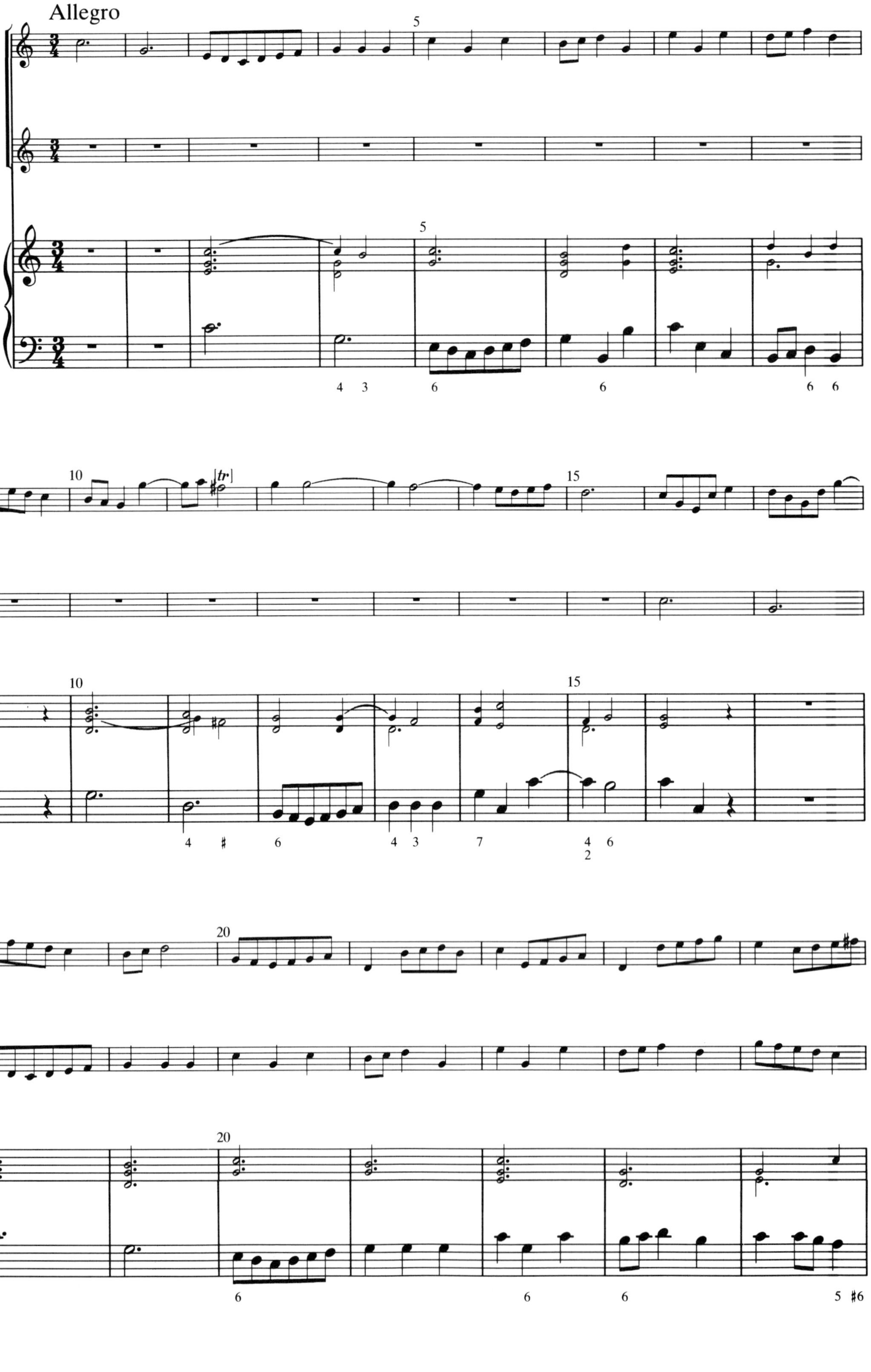
Allegro
tr

83

84

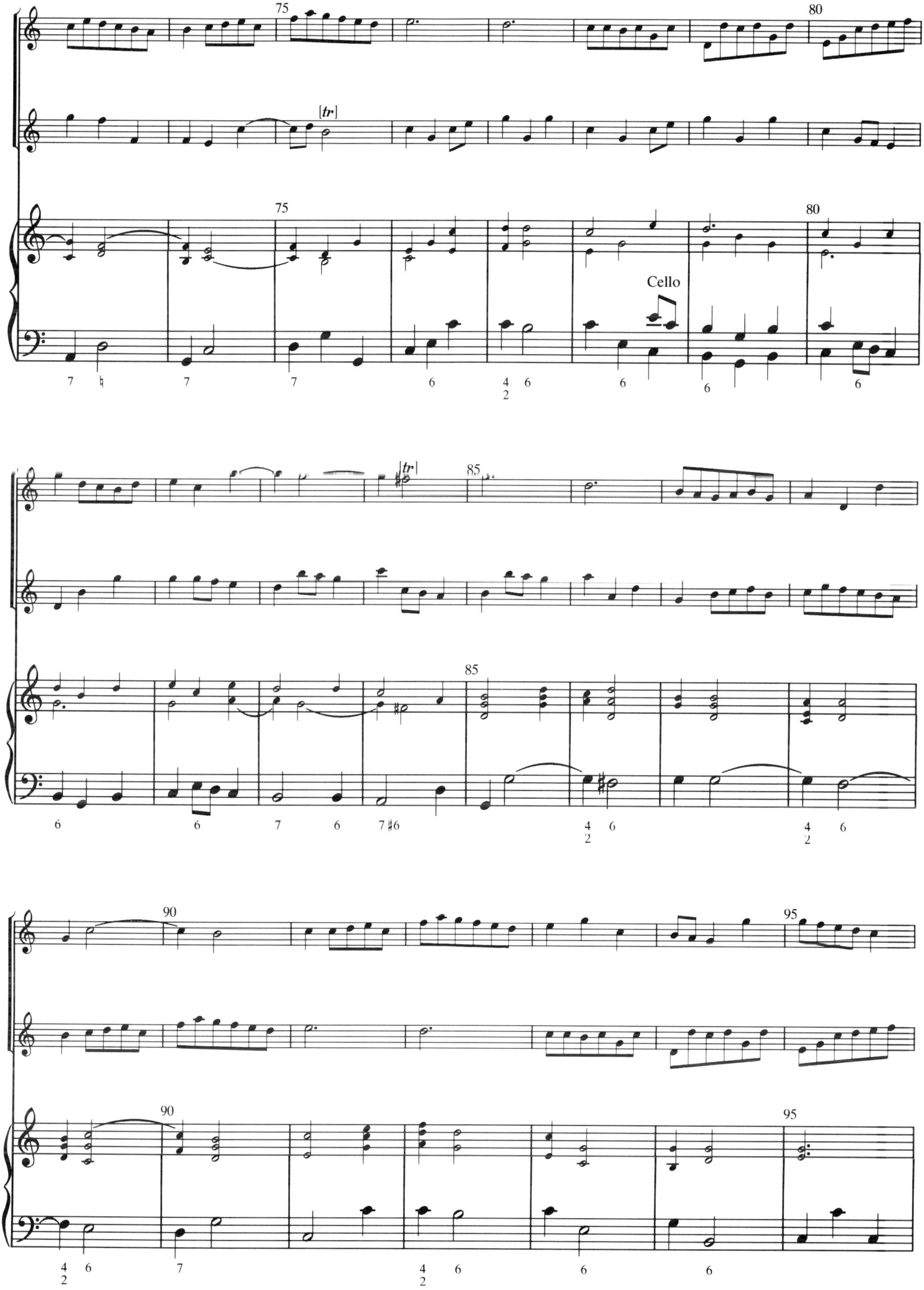
75
[tr]
80
Cello
85
[tr]
90
95

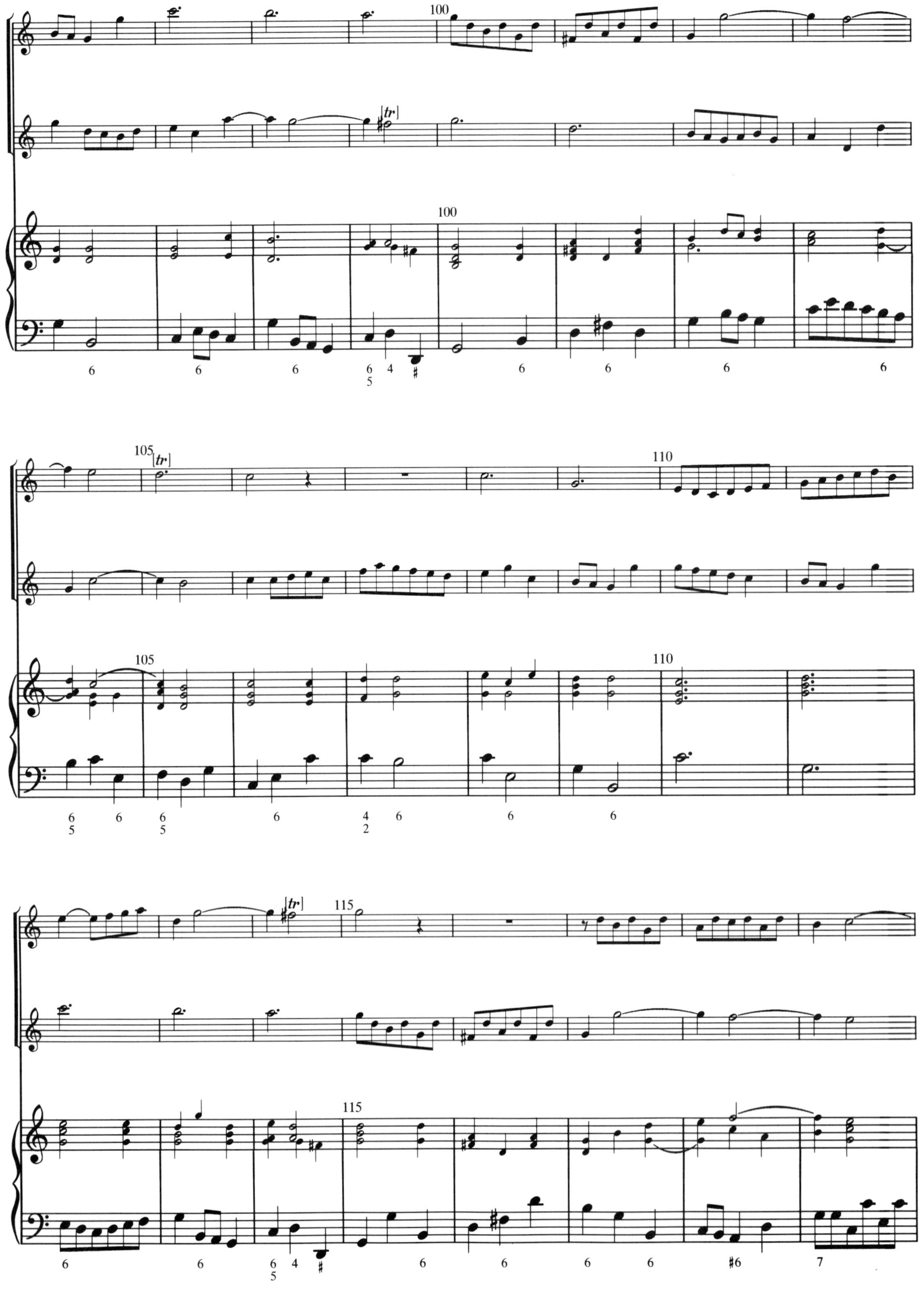
100
[tr]
105
110
115

87

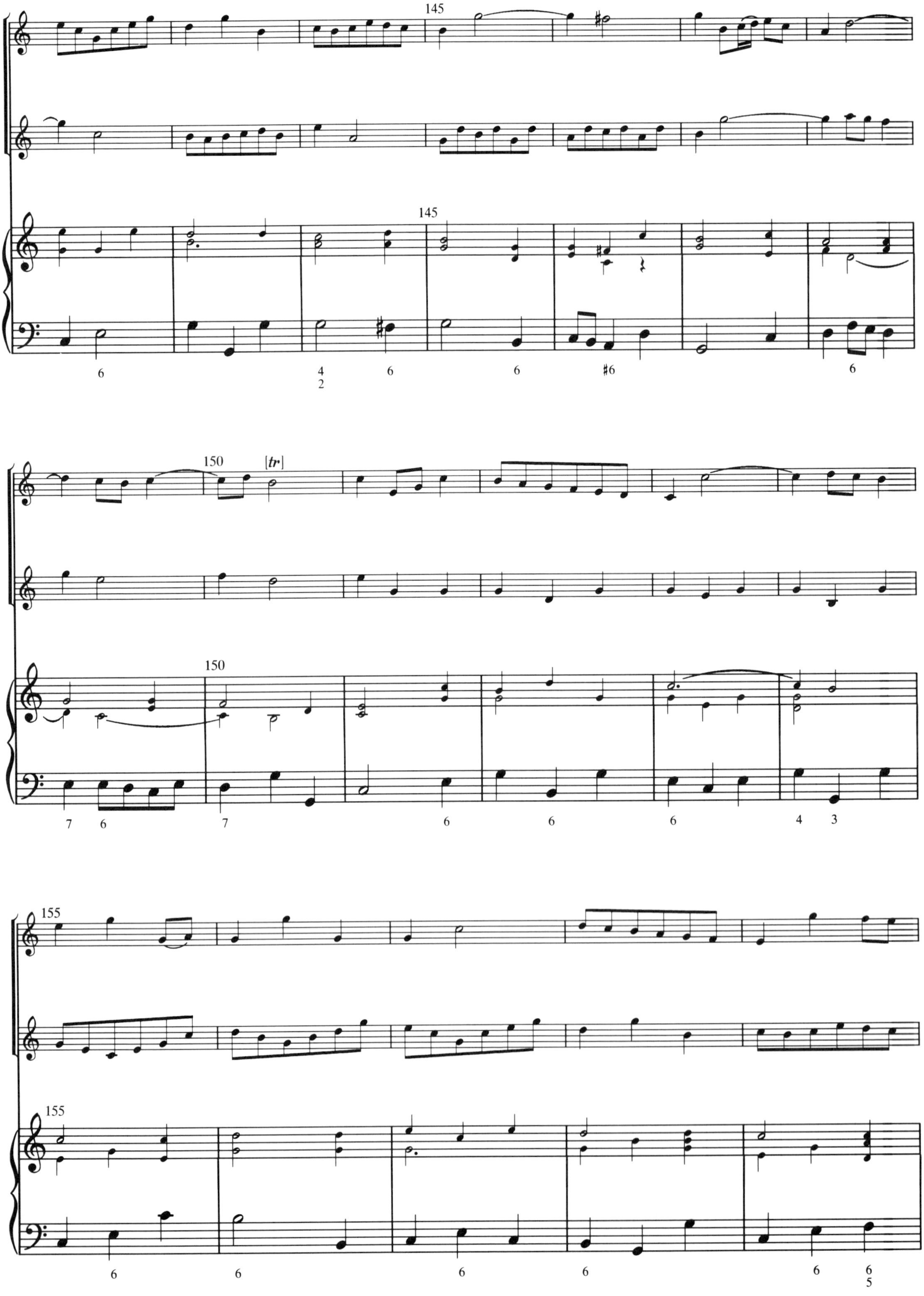

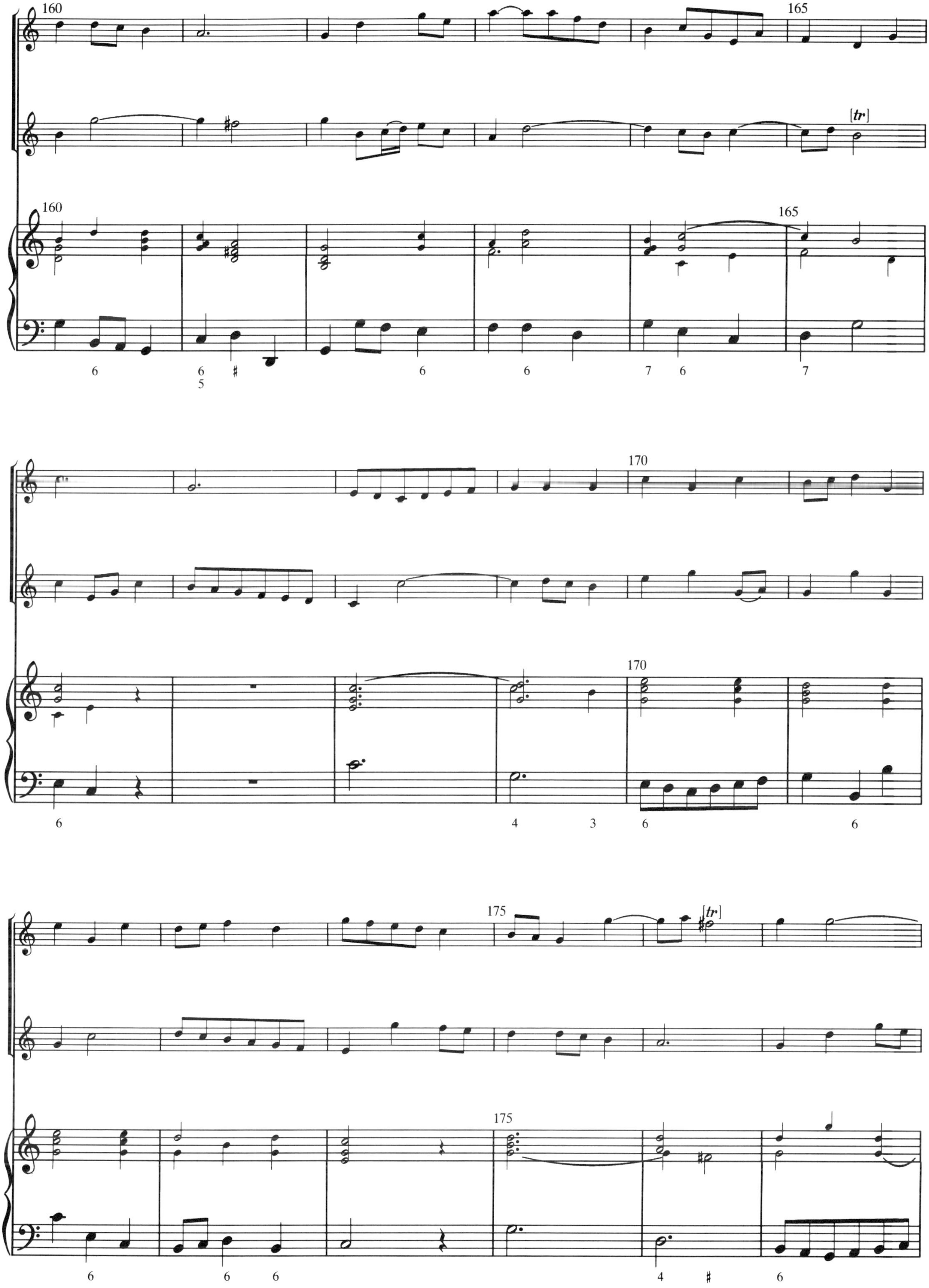
160
165
[tr]
170
175
[tr]

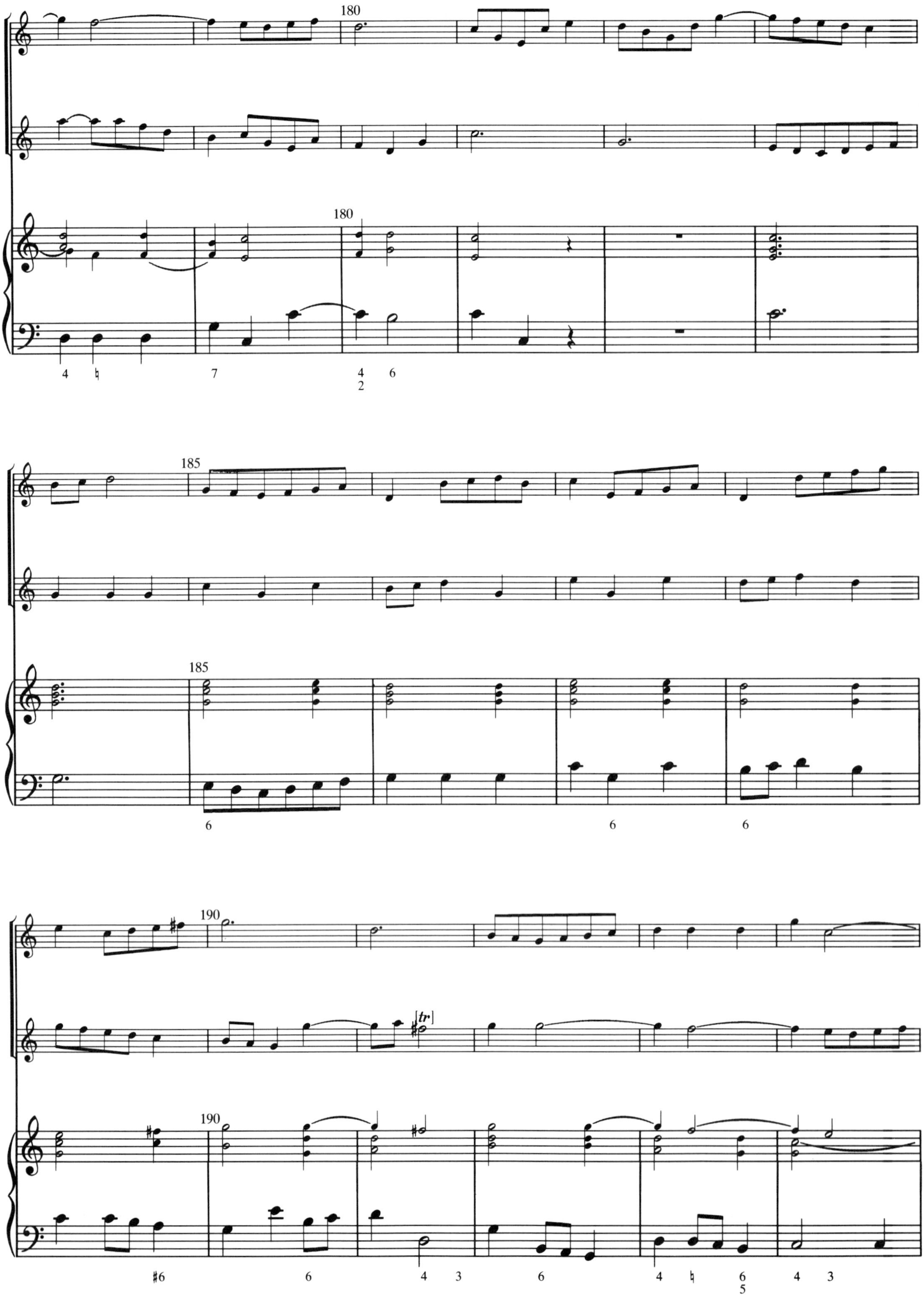
180
185
190
[tr]

91

Suite III

ALLEMANDA
Allegretto

93

94

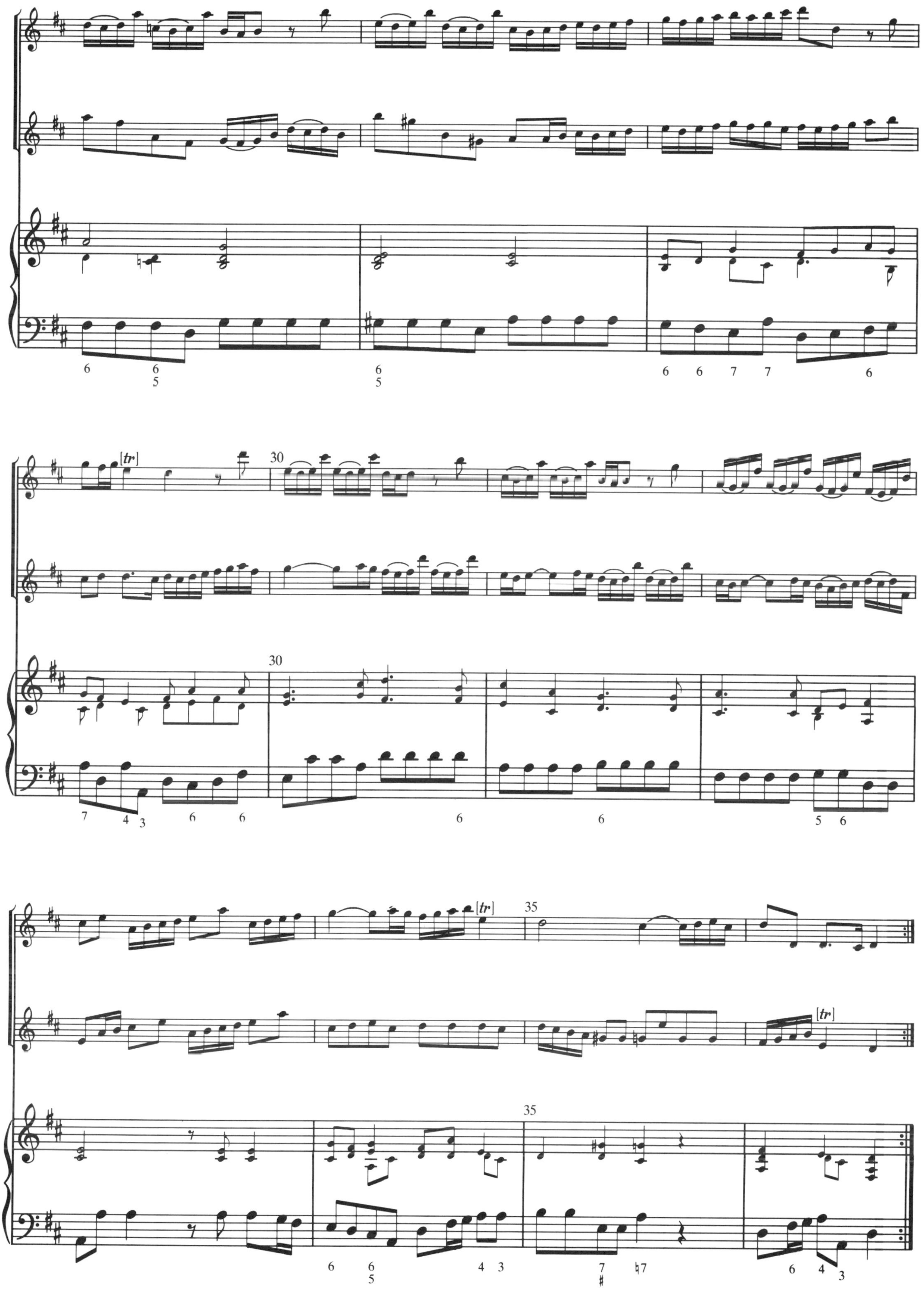
[tr]
30
35

GIGA
Allegro

97

98

99

SARABANDA
Allegro

101

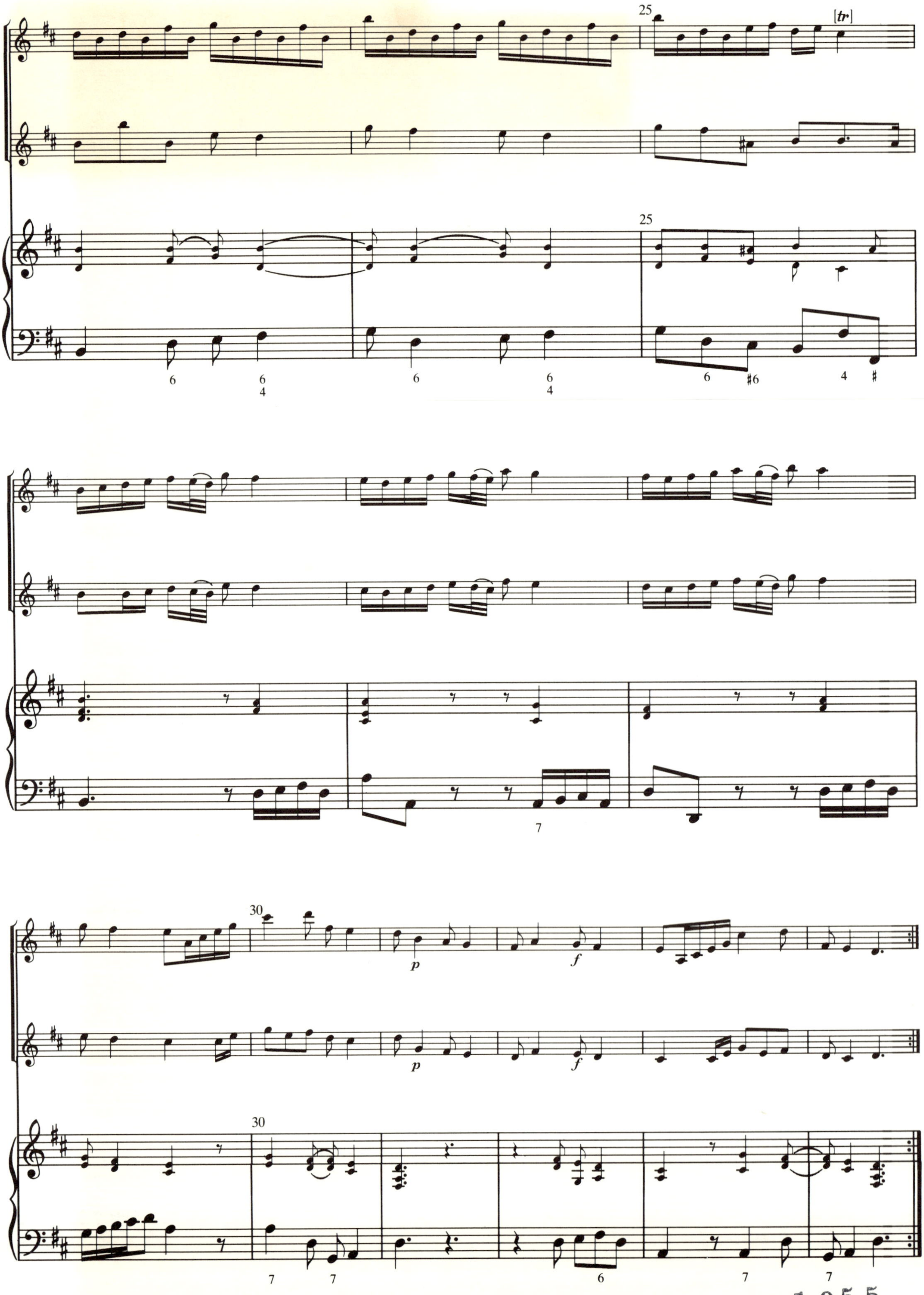
25
[tr]
30
p
f